WOMEN IN HISTORY

Women of the Vietnam War

Mark Schynert

LUCENT BOOKS

An imprint of Thomson Gale, a part of The Thomson Corporation

Detroit • New York • San Francisco • San Diego • New Haven, Conn. • Waterville, Maine • London • Munich

© 2005 Thomson Gale, a part of the Thomson Corporation.

Thomson and Star Logo are trademarks and Gale and Lucent Books are registered trademarks used herein under license.

For more information, contact
Lucent Books
27500 Drake Rd.
Farmington Hills, MI 48331-3535
Or you can visit our Internet site at http://www.gale.com

LIBRARY OF CONGRESS CATALOGING-IN-PUBLICATION DATA

Schynert, Mark, 1952–
    Women of the Vietnam War / by Mark Schynert.
        p. cm. — (Women in history)
Includes bibliographical references and index.
    ISBN 1-59018-474-2 (hardcover : alk. paper)
    [1. Vietnamese Conflict, 1961–1975—Women—Juvenile literature.] I. Title. II. Series:
Women in history (San Diego, Calif.)
    DS559.8.W6S39 2004
    959.704'3'082--dc22
                                                    2004010208

Printed in the United States of America

Contents

Foreword

The story of the past as told in traditional historical writings all too often leaves the impression that if men are not the only actors in the narrative, they are assuredly the main characters. With a few notable exceptions, males were the political, military, and economic leaders in virtually every culture throughout recorded time. Since traditional historical scholarship focuses on the public arenas of government, foreign relations, and commerce, the actions and ideas of men—or at least of powerful men—are naturally at the center of conventional accounts of the past.

In the last several decades, however, many historians have abandoned their predecessors' emphasis on "great men" to explore the past "from the bottom up," a phenomenon that has had important consequences for the study of women's history. These social historians, as they are known, focus on the day-to-day experiences of the "silent majority"—those people typically omitted from conventional scholarship because they held relatively little political or economic sway within their societies. In the new social history, members of ethnic and racial minorities, factory workers, peasants, slaves, children,

and women are no longer relegated to the background but are placed at the very heart of the narrative.

Around the same time social historians began broadening their research to include women and other previously neglected elements of society, the feminist movement of the late 1960s and 1970s was also bringing unprecedented attention to the female heritage. Feminists hoped that by examining women's past experiences, contemporary women could better understand why and how gender-based expectations had developed in their societies, as well as how they might reshape inherited—and typically restrictive—economic, social, and political roles in the future.

Today, some four decades after the feminist and social history movements gave new impetus to the study of women's history, there is a rich and continually growing body of work on all aspects of women's lives in the past. The Lucent Books Women in History series draws upon this abundant and diverse literature to introduce students to women's experiences within a variety of past cultures and time periods in terms of the distinct roles they filled. In their capacities as workers, activists, and artists, women exerted significant influence on important events whether they conformed to or broke from traditional roles. The Women in History titles depict extraordinary women who managed to attain positions of influence in their male-dominated societies, including such celebrated heroines as the feisty medieval queen Eleanor of Aquitaine, the brilliant propagandist of the American Revolution Mercy Otis Warren, and the courageous African American activist of the Civil War era Harriet Tubman. Included as well are the stories of the ordinary—and often overlooked—women of the past who also helped shape their societies myriad ways—moral, intellectual, and economic—without straying far from customary gender roles: the housewives and mothers, schoolteachers and church volunteers, midwives and nurses and wartime camp followers.

In this series, readers will discover that many of these unsung women took more significant parts in the great political and social upheavals of their day than has often been recognized. In *Women of the American Revolution,* for example, students will learn how American housewives assumed a crucial role in helping the Patriots win the war against Britain. They accomplished this by planting and harvesting fields, producing and trading goods, and doing whatever else was necessary to maintain the family farm or business in the absence of their soldier husbands despite the heavy burden of housekeeping and child-care duties they already bore. By their self-sacrificing actions, competence, and ingenuity, these anonymous heroines not only kept their families alive, but kept the economy of their struggling young nation going as well during eight long years of war.

Each volume in this series contains generous commentary from the works of respected contemporary scholars, but the Women in History series particularly emphasizes quotations from primary sources such as diaries, letters, and journals whenever possible to allow the women of the past to speak for themselves. These firsthand accounts not only help students to better understand the dimensions of women's daily spheres—the work they did, the organizations they belonged to, the physical hardships they faced—but also how they viewed themselves and their actions in the light of their society's expectations for their sex.

The distinguished American historian Mary Beard once wrote that women have always been a "force in history." It is hoped that the books in this series will help students to better appreciate the vital yet often little-known ways in which women of the past have shaped their societies and cultures.

Introduction:
The War and the Women

It is difficult to give an exact date for the start of the Vietnam War. At the root of the conflict was Vietnamese desire to be free of foreign control. Vietnam had a long history of independence, stretching back over two thousand years, but in 1863 French imperialists established a colony in the south part of Vietnam. The Vietnamese emperor tried to resist French influence, but failed. France conquered all of Vietnam by 1887.

From the start, the Vietnamese rebelled against the French. Nevertheless, the French dominated Vietnam. They even abolished the name. They referred to Vietnam in three parts—Tonkin, Annam, and Cochin China—and to the whole as part of French Indochina, which also included Cambodia and Laos. The French called the Vietnamese themselves Annamites.

Japan ended French rule in Vietnam in 1940, right before the start of World War II in Asia and the Pacific. The French were kept as puppet rulers, but the Japanese made the decisions. During the war the Japanese ruthlessly exploited the Vietnamese. They took so much food from Vietnam for their own purposes that they caused a famine in 1945.

When World War II ended in 1945, a popular leader of the northern Vietnamese, Ho Chi Minh, sought help from the United States to restore Vietnamese independence. However, he was devoted to communism, a social and political doctrine based on abolishing differences in wealth and status in society. The United States and its allies, which included France, are capitalist countries. After World War II, capitalist countries came to view communism as a major threat to worldwide peace and security. This tension evolved into the Cold War (a global confrontation between democracy and communism that usually stopped just short of combat).

Thus, the United States ultimately did not support Ho Chi Minh because he was a Communist, and instead supported French rule in Vietnam. The Vietnamese, however, resisted the French. The Viet Minh, as the northern Communists called themselves, began engaging the

French in full-scale combat and inflicted a major defeat on them in 1954. A truce followed and Vietnam was partitioned in 1956 into North Vietnam, controlled by the Viet Minh, and South Vietnam, ruled by the last emperor of Vietnam, Bao Dai.

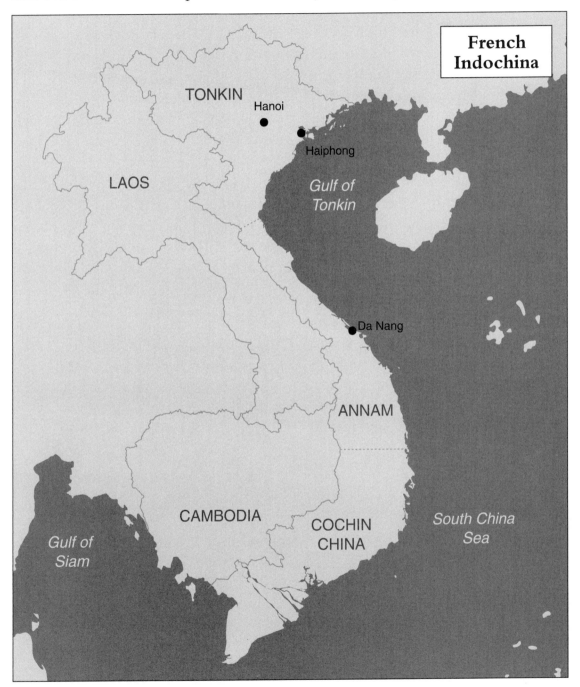

Under the terms of the truce, an election was to be held to unify Vietnam under one leader. It never took place, however; the Americans and the South Vietnamese regime feared that Ho Chi Minh would be elected and a Communist state declared throughout Vietnam, and so prevented elections. Because their desire to unify the country had been thwarted, North Vietnam began to support guerrilla warriors (plainclothes soldiers who often committed acts of terrorism in the south) called Viet Cong (*Cong* means "Communist" in Vietnamese). Meanwhile, the United States began to send military advisers (soldiers who train local troops) to help capitalist South Vietnam defend itself.

In 1964, after a naval engagement known as the Tonkin Gulf Incident, the United States escalated its involvement in the conflict. In the context of the Cold War, U.S. policy makers considered it necessary to stop communism from being established in Vietnam, for fear that all the other countries in Indochina would fall to communism in succession. Thus, hundreds of thousands of U.S. troops were in Vietnam by 1967, as well as soldiers from Australia and several other countries. Targets in both North and South Vietnam were subjected to American air raids and naval artillery bombardments.

Many people on both sides were killed and injured, and much property

South Vietnamese women and children take cover in a canal from enemy fire. The Vietnam War profoundly affected the lives of Vietnamese women and the women of South Vietnam's Western allies.

was destroyed. Nevertheless, the war went on without a conclusion in sight. Like the French before, the American people decided they had had enough. The United States withdrew its military from South Vietnam under a truce negotiated in 1973; the South Vietnamese took over their own defense. However, the South Vietnamese could not resist on their own. Saigon, the South Vietnamese capital, fell in April 1975. The fall of Saigon marked the end of the Vietnam War.

The Women Affected

The Vietnam War involved two distinct communities of women and affected them in very different ways. One group of women was part of an agricultural society, where their roles traditionally centered on the family and on farming. Indeed, more than 80 percent of the female population of Vietnam lived as peasants. The second group of women, the women of the Western allies of South Vietnam, and most especially women from America and Australia, was far more diverse in wealth, cultural background, education, and beliefs.

This war influenced many women profoundly. Most directly affected along with Vietnamese women were others who went to Vietnam during the war. By one estimate, about twenty thousand foreign women were in Vietnam during the war. About fifteen thousand were Americans, and another thousand were Australians. A few were injured or killed. Most went home with experiences they never would have had otherwise, many with great emotional weight.

Women in America and Australia were also affected, as these countries sent troops to Vietnam. Women were among the first to oppose the war and the military draft in both countries. In America, women's participation contributed to the women's movement, with its focus on equal rights and opportunity. Women were also essential to the Australian antiwar movement, and their participation led to political awakening for women in Australia.

For Vietnamese women, the war was far more than a controversial or tragic conflict; it was a national nightmare. Those who lived through it often lost material possessions—homes, goods, and money. Many lost families. Many were injured or killed. North Vietnamese women had been required to radically change their roles in society, undertaking jobs traditionally reserved for men and risking their lives in combat. Although different groups of women were affected by the war in different ways, all were changed by the experience, and these changes were reflected in women's roles in Vietnam, America, and Australia after the war.

Chapter 1:
The Vietnamese
Home Fronts

The Vietnam War was for the most part a war without well-defined battle zones, which meant that the home fronts were sometimes also the front lines. Viet Cong guerrillas might strike anywhere in South Vietnam at any time, and South Vietnamese or American attacks on Communist targets put many Vietnamese both in the north and south at risk. South Vietnamese women often found their homes became part of the battleground, which put them and their families in peril. Many others were forced from their homes permanently and became refugees.

Many women in the south had to adapt to changing roles simply to survive or to take care of their families. In the north many women held more than one role at once, performing their normal jobs part of the time and helping to defend against air raids or deal with the damage and injury afterward. North Vietnamese women also took on traditionally male roles and conducted their lives in ways that challenged long-standing cultural expectations.

Peasant Women in South Vietnam

More than 80 percent of the women in South Vietnam were peasants. They spent long days working in the fields and caring for children. A few peasant women added to family earnings with small businesses, such as noodle stands, but that was in addition to their traditional responsibilities. At best, the life of peasants was arduous, and it became very difficult when crops were poor. As one peasant woman, Nguyen Thi Lan, said, "If the crops are good, I can make ends meet. If not, I have to beg the landlord to lower the rent and borrow some money so that my family will have enough to eat."[1]

The effects of war could be devastating for these women. Peasants might be killed or injured, and their livestock, crops, and homes could be destroyed. South Vietnamese in the countryside were often caught in battle between Viet Cong (Communist irregular soldiers who fought for North Vietnam, also called guerrillas or insurgents) and government or allied troops.

Even when men were hurt, women still suffered, because in Vietnamese society, women had the conditions of their life defined by the men in their life: fathers, husbands, and sons. A woman who lost her husband or her sons also lost her place in society, and thus was further challenged to provide for her family. For example, widows of soldiers of the South Vietnamese Army of the Republic of Vietnam (ARVN) were entitled to a pension, but the men's own officers frequently stole these pensions, leaving the widows with no compensation. There was no pension at all for the widow of a Viet Cong. In either event, women were forced to scramble to sustain their family. They either found refuge with extended family members or would have to take the most menial of jobs, such as street peddling.

Keeping the Family Together

The most important goal of most Vietnamese women was to maintain their family even when times were difficult. During the war, impoverished South Vietnamese women would sell anything they could to those who had money: their own possessions from better times, catfish and eels they caught in nearby rivers, snacks or drinks, or black market cigarettes. The heartier among them might also cut and haul firewood for sale. Some women found work in the

fields of landowners, but the wages they received were low; women were paid much less than men for farmwork.

Even the most prosperous peasant women in the south often faced similar problems if their men were fighting either for the ARVN or the Viet Cong. Most peasant men who became soldiers naturally had to forsake their farmwork. Any woman left behind thus had to pick up the pieces; if she stayed in her hamlet

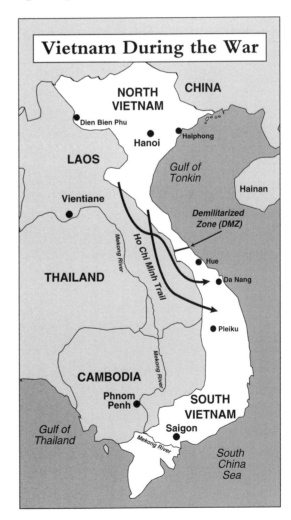

The Ancient Status of Vietnamese Women

❧

In the 1950s Vietnamese women were expected to be subservient to men. This was a long-standing expectation, rooted in the Confucian doctrine imposed by the Chinese when they first conquered Vietnam. Prior to the Chinese invasion about two thousand years ago, Vietnam had been a matriarchal society; women were honored in legend and literature. The female married at will, whereupon her husband had to move to her home.

During the thousand or so years of Chinese rule, Vietnamese women were expected to submit to the Three Obediences of Confucian doctrine: to their father, their husband, and their son. In essence, a woman's life was defined primarily by the men in her life. Certainly many people were in loving and happy marriages, but many women were also mistreated by their husbands. The prac-

tice of polygamy (men with more than one wife) was common where the man could afford it, which reduced the less-favored wives to little more than drudges. Wives could be discarded at will, yet had no right to divorce a husband. These rules only began to change in the 1960s, and more quickly in the Communist north than in the Republic of South Vietnam. The attitudes of most people changed even more slowly.

Vietnamese women did have some significant rights. They could traditionally inherit land, serve as trustees of ancestral cults, and share their husbands' property. In this regard, they were better off than the women of any other nation in Asia. Still, a Vietnamese woman had to contend with the deeply held notion that if she did not keep her place, her actions would harm not just her family, but society itself.

(a small village or part of a village complex), she took on heavier labor usually done by men to keep up with the crops, while also performing her usual family-related tasks.

For some women, keeping the family together was only possible if they left their home villages. In order to maintain a semblance of family, many women and children of South Vietnamese soldiers fol-

lowed their men from post to post, living in tent cities if need be. Others found better housing, but still had a hard time sustaining their families with limited income and increased expenses. For example, Private Pham Van Loc's wife and children moved to a nearby city to be close to him while he was in the ARVN. Loc sent her about twenty dollars a month from his pay, but that was barely enough to make ends meet. As she knew only farming, his wife could not get a job in the city; with no relatives at hand to help with child care, she had to take care of their two small children all day. Loc described the difference between their lives during the war and their lives at home: "In [our] own hamlet, we would both work in the rice fields. . . . [We] would build [our] own home and pay no rent. . . . At home, [we] would have better clothes and medical care, and . . . save [five or ten dollars] a month."[2]

Peasant women in South Vietnam also kept the family together by caring for injured or ill family members, even by following them to hospitals. Hospital care in South Vietnam was very limited due to shortages of medical personnel, beds, and supplies. Often, the only food supplied by the hospital was rice. Beale Rodgers, an American doctor working in a small South Vietnamese hospital, recalls that "for the most part, nursing care and food and everything was provided by the family."[3]

Even when South Vietnamese were treated in U.S. Army hospitals and had access to more sophisticated services, the families still looked after their ill and

A U.S. Army nurse takes a wounded baby from the mother's arms. South Vietnamese women often insisted on accompanying injured family members to the hospital.

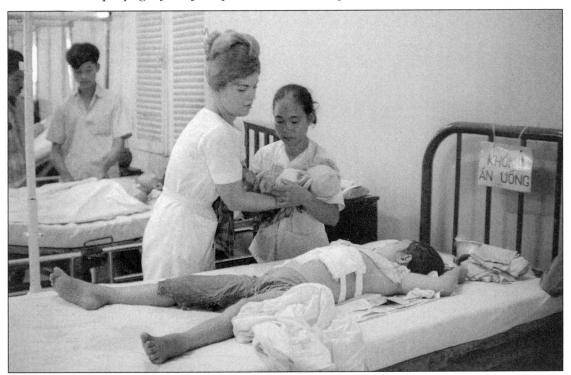

injured. Army nurse Sharon Lane wrote, "The sickest [Vietnamese] have a family member with them who bathes them and feeds them."[4] Those working at the Australian military hospital at Vung Tau saw their Vietnamese patients attended by female relatives. According to Australian writer Siobhan McHugh, "Families literally camped by the bedside . . . they cooked up meals on primus stoves, fed, washed and changed dressings . . . and slept in or under the patient's bed. If a child was ill, a grandmother or aunt was by its side day and night, while the mother cared for the other children at home."[5]

Keeping the family together came to be even more of a challenge for many women during the middle and later stages of the war, as American and ARVN forces evacuated whole villages. The villages and all the surrounding crops were burned to deny food and shelter to Viet Cong in the area. Defoliants (plant-killing chemicals) were often used as well, killing off all the surrounding vegetation, often for years. These disruptions displaced many peasants and their families. About a quarter of the country's population became refugees who flowed into the major cities. There they were forced to live in squalid conditions. Families became destitute and resorted to begging and garbage picking.

Bar Girls, Prostitutes, and Romantic Attachments

Vietnamese girls and young women soon saw other opportunities, though. The easiest way for girls or young women to make money during the Vietnam War was to seek out American men, who to them seemed unimaginably rich. As historian Stanley Karnow puts it, "[The] children [of the refugees], tempted by the incredible affluence that the Americans had brought to Vietnam, defied time-honored vows of filial piety [obedience to parental wishes] and broke away from their parents in a quest for easy wealth."[6] Soldiers on leave, or other foreign men, lonely for feminine affection, went to bars in the cities, where they purchased watered-down, overpriced liquor or tea from bar girls. The bar girls kept the men company for fifteen to thirty minutes per beverage. The bar girls got half the price of each beverage, with the rest going to the bar's owner. As each beverage cost several dollars, a bar girl could easily make more money in one evening than a peasant could earn from working in the fields for a week.

Some bar girls also engaged in prostitution, although it was not their primary occupation. Bill Crownover, a civilian electrical technician in Vietnam during the war, says of the bar girls at Mimi's, a Saigon bar he frequented:

Defoliants

The Viet Cong and the North Vietnamese depended on the rain forests of Vietnam to provide cover from American air power. They also relied on the harvests from these forests to supply a large part of their food. Part of the American strategy for hampering the Communist insurgents was to use defoliants to kill off the forests and the crops, leaving the guerrillas with less shelter and food.

To this end, the United States sprayed large quantities of chemical defoliants. Three chemical sprays were widely used. The most notorious was known as Agent Orange. Sprayed from aircraft, it destroyed many square miles of Vietnamese jungle by causing all the leaves on the trees, bushes, and vines to wither and fall off. Most plants were immediately killed by the spray, while the few survivors were stunted and grew back very slowly.

Agent Orange also had unexpected long-term effects. It persists in the environment for years and causes cancer, birth defects, and genetic damage, as well as other medical problems. Statistics showed a large number of birth defects after the war for Vietnamese children and the children of Australians and Americans who went to Vietnam. It is probable Agent Orange caused most of these problems; many women were affected, directly or indirectly, even long after the war ended.

"They weren't prostitutes, not in the normal sense of the word. They weren't for hire to anyone who walked in. . . . They might [prostitute themselves] for [a lot] of money. But it just wasn't their regular line of work . . . most of [them] had one or two special customers."[7]

Many women were solely prostitutes. Indeed, about three hundred thousand women and girls turned to prostitution in South Vietnam during the war. They worked in strip clubs, massage parlors, and brothels, or simply cruised on the back seat of their manager's motorcycle, looking for business. Many contracted venereal diseases and could not always get effective treatment for the illnesses. Many also became pregnant. Most supported their families with their earnings, which was often the only significant income the family had. Prostitutes charged between fifteen and two hundred dollars per customer. Even when they had to split the money with someone else, such as their pimp, they often made more money than did bar girls.

Despite prostitution's illegality, the South Vietnamese government usually looked the other way. Madame Ngo Dinh Nhu, the powerful sister-in-law of President Ngo Dinh Diem, used her political influence in the early 1960s to try to ban or limit the sex trade, but she had little impact. American authorities also did little to stop prostitution. In fact, at least one brothel was set up right on an American base. Ingrid Hart, an Australian entertainer who performed for allied troops in Vietnam, said, "[A] Vietnamese woman persuaded the Americans that a legalised brothel within Long Binh base would be safer all around. . . . Everything was [gold-plated], the food was excellent, it was the most beautiful Chinese pagoda in the middle of an army camp."[8]

Some South Vietnamese women approached prostitution in a more casual manner. They might develop a relationship with a Western man, and then over time ask for monetary gifts to help meet living expenses. They might even ask for loans which neither party ever expected to be paid back. Robin Pell, an

Vietnamese prostitutes wait for customers. Although the practice was illegal, prostitution proved very lucrative for many Vietnamese women during the war.

Women of the Vietnam War

American working for the U.S. Agency for International Development, recalls the custom: "You just went down to the bars and picked out a girl and took her home and it cost you a certain amount of money . . . sometimes girls [would] come home with you for nothing. Later on it got more and more commercial. Then there were in-between areas, where a girl would be sort of your girlfriend but occasionally hit you up for money."[9]

Some women had mixed feelings about their relationships with American men. For example, when she learned of the planned American pullout from South Vietnam in 1971, twenty-three-year-old Mai spoke of the American soldier who fathered her two children. "Before, he want to marry me and I say 'no.' I want to stay here. . . . Now, I want. But now be too late. He gone."[10]

Others had no doubt; they wanted to marry Americans. The role of wife and mother appealed to them, especially if it meant a way out of the war. Many wanted a way to get to the United States, an affluent society, especially compared to impoverished Vietnam. One American embassy worker said, "A lot of girls ended up with very lonely American GIs (soldiers) who suddenly found themselves the idol of someone else's attention. . . . How these things resolved themselves once they got back

to the [United] States I don't know. But ninety percent or more of the relationships ended when the plane left with the American on it going home."[11] Many romances never became marriages, even if children were born to the couple while they were together in Vietnam. Some did get married, though; American men who were legally married brought their wives and any children out of Vietnam and back to the United States.

Mama-Sans

While many Vietnamese women made a living off of relationships with American men, others were not so inclined, or were not young enough to do so. Americans in Vietnam had other needs as well, though. Many women became mama-sans to meet these needs and earn money. *Mama-san* was a colloquial term Americans used primarily to describe female Vietnamese domestic helpers. The term covered a wide range of roles, from women who did laundry or polished boots for Western men and women, to housekeepers and even live-in mistresses.

Thousands of women secured identification cards from the U.S. Army and came onto bases to polish boots and perform other cleaning services. Some on-base mama-sans had unusual jobs. James Hagenkizer, a medic assigned to

A young mama-san, or domestic servant, shines boots for U.S. soldiers.

an army field hospital on the coast, recounted, "In the afternoon, everyone would go to the beach. You lay on the beach and the mamasans came around and sold pineapples and bananas and Coca Cola."[12] Others worked as nurse's aides in the U.S. Army hospitals. Indi-

vidual soldiers also paid mama-sans to do laundry, picking from among the many Vietnamese women who lived in shantytowns just outside major military bases.

The mama-sans on military bases were not always trustworthy. Army nurse Sharon Lane, for example, complained that "you can have your mama-san launder your clothes but [the other nurses] say you only get half of them back—especially if you wear small sizes. She keeps whatever she likes. So I have my bathing suit and some other stuff locked in my duffel bag."[13] On the other hand, some mama-sans not only were honest, but befriended their employers. Several Western women were even invited to meet a mama-san's family. On such occasions, the families treated the Westerners as the most honored of guests, and went to great effort to extend every possible hospitality.

Since many of the mama-sans gained access to American military installations, they could be a security risk. In fact, they were often suspected of being informants for Communist guerrillas, and many mama-sans seemed to know when a Viet Cong attack was expected. Lane wrote, "Usually [the mama-sans] get wind of impending attacks and don't come in on those days . . . some are suspected to be either [Viet Cong] or VC supporters."[14] At least one U.S. Army general would not allow Vietnamese women on base. Lieutenant General Harry Kinnard suspected that if women worked at his base camp (a fortified area for troops), they would pass information on the layout of the camp to the Viet Cong. "I wouldn't let any Vietnamese . . . inside the barrier. . . . No cooks, no laundry women, no [prostitutes], no nothing. . . . And because of that, we were never accurately [attacked with mortar shells]." [15]

Both soldiers and civilians found it convenient to hire a mama-san to keep house for them. Some soldiers lived off base, and there were also many Western civilians in Vietnam doing business with the U.S. forces or the Vietnamese government, or working on behalf of some other organization. Reporters, contractors, and businessmen often stayed in Vietnam for a year or more. All of these Americans could hire a mama-san to deal with all domestic tasks for a very low salary by Western reckoning, though a good wage by Vietnamese standards.

Some men developed romantic attachments with their mama-sans; others took mama-sans as mistresses without forming an emotional bond. Television war correspondent Liz Trotta notes how these relationships ended with many of her male colleagues: "Once the newsman was transferred [home], the [mama-san] was passed on to a friend or simply dumped amid rash promises to return and reclaim her as a bride . . . [although] some did marry their girlfriends and take them back to the states." [16]

Some Vietnamese people were offended to see young Vietnamese women living openly with American men without getting married, but others were tolerant of the practice. One landlord, Vu Van Phan, rented apartments to several couples of American soldiers and Vietnamese girls. He referred to the girls as concubines, a derogatory term by Vietnamese standards, but went on to say, "The concubines aren't bad girls. . . . All of the girls help support their families. . . . They love their men even though there have been no wedding ceremonies. . . . They're always welcome to eat with us. They're just like elder sisters to my children." [17]

Drugs and Black Marketeering

While some Vietnamese women established relationships with Americans as bar girls, prostitutes, or mama-sans, others made a living selling merchandise. During the war many women sold legitimate goods of every sort, but illegal goods were much more profitable. Women sold marijuana, heroin, opium, and other drugs to Americans. About half of all American troops used illegal drugs at least occasionally, and drug use was also common among Western civilians in Vietnam. By American standards, these illegal drugs were both cheap and plentiful, but the sale of drugs was very lucrative and demand was high.

Sale of these drugs was against the law in Vietnam, but the law was rarely enforced. Street vendors in the cities openly sold marijuana. As war correspondent Denby Fawcett wrote, "[In Saigon], I always stopped to visit an elderly Vietnamese woman selling second-hand paperback books from her street stand. The lady proudly showed me sealed packs of [a popular brand of cigarette], but the filtered cigarettes inside were marijuana joints, . . . $2.50 a pack."[18] Drug dealers could also be found outside all major military bases, where a marijuana cigarette might cost as little as a dime.

Drugs were not the only illicit goods women sold. Vast quantities of merchandise were stolen from the American or South Vietnamese armies, redirected by corrupt Vietnamese officials, or misappropriated from the U.S. Post Exchange (PX) system. Many items found their way into the black market, an illegal, underground market where almost anything could be bought. A U.S. Army military policeman spoke of one incident that highlighted women's activity in black market sales. "I was involved in an orphanage assistance program. . . . We arranged . . . to have a truck that the nuns could bring in [to the base supply depot] and get old stuff that wasn't being used. . . . [The] nuns were stopped on the way out with a truckload of [modern electronic equipment] headed straight for the black market."[19]

In some cases, women were so desperate to make money they denied themselves necessary items. For example, Americans often supplied starving Vietnamese women with C rations, canned food carried by soldiers in the field. Instead of using the C rations themselves, the women sold the food on the black market, where it was in demand, and used the cash for rice and other necessities. Although they were starving, the C rations were worth too much to eat; the women were able to get much more food with the cash they got from selling the rations.

Many female merchants sold legitimate and stolen goods side by side, often at prices better than the PX could offer. Sales of pilfered tobacco products and liquor were especially popular. Despite the illegality of the black market, no one made a secret of it. Women did not make as much money with black market sales as they might with prostitution or drug sales, but their income was still substantial. It was also probably a safer way to make a living, since these women did not run the risk of venereal disease that prostitutes had to face, nor the risk of theft or violence by drug users or competing sellers.

Women in North Vietnam

Most women in North Vietnam were peasants and held the same traditional roles as did women in the south. However, between 1954 and 1960 most landowners in the north were executed or had their land confiscated by the Communist regime, and most farmland was held by peasants' collectives. The existence of collectives probably made women's lives a little easier, as there was more communal support than in South Vietnam, where a woman could count only on her own family.

When the United States escalated its involvement in Vietnam in 1964, however, the roles of North Vietnamese women substantially changed. The Americans' combat effectiveness, far greater than that of ARVN troops, caused Viet Cong and North Vietnamese Army (NVA) casualties to rise. At the same time, the American air raids brought the war to North Vietnam. There were simply not enough men to replace combat casualties, repair roads and bridges, defuse bombs, operate anti-aircraft defenses, search for downed

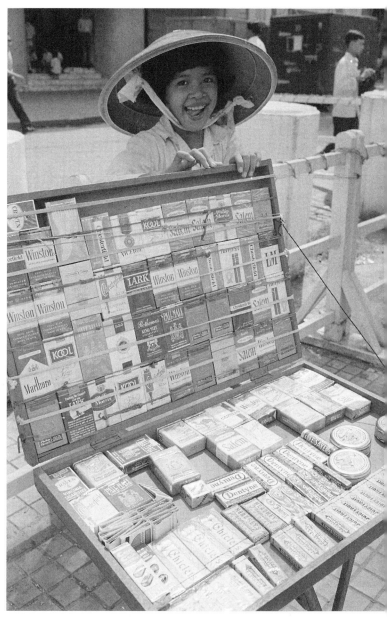

A South Vietnamese woman in Saigon sells cigarettes, candy, and other American goods on the black market.

enemy pilots, move supplies south to the Viet Cong, and keep factories and fields productive. Historian Jon M. Van Dyke writes,

A North Vietnamese girl takes target practice with her militia unit. North Vietnam strongly encouraged women to join militia units, some of which saw combat.

The response of the North Vietnamese was to formulate the Three Responsibilities Movement. The Vietnam Women's Union urged women to do the following:

(1) Replace the men who were called from the fields and factories for combat duties.

(2) Take charge of their families, so that husbands could leave for the front, knowing that the family would be well taken care of.

(3) Join militia units to take part in combat when necessary.[20]

The intent was to keep production levels up and to ease the minds of the men at the front, but it also suddenly increased opportunities for women. The number of women in the workforce aside from agriculture grew dramatical-

Women of the Vietnam War

ly; one source notes an increase from 348,000 in 1965 to about 1.3 million in 1967. All the professions, from physician to engineer to teacher, were open to women now; but as a practical matter, there were few opportunities for those with limited education. The war situation dictated a focus on production: food, clothing, weapons, and tools.

Almost every able-bodied young man was by then enlisted; women flocked to fill all the other jobs as best they could. Women built schools and dormitories with little more than bamboo. "We had no equipment," said North Vietnamese film actress Duc Hoan. "Everything useful went to the armies and so we had to use conical [straw] hats to carry dirt—each one holds two kilograms and they worked quite well."[21] Women worked in mines, and knitted clothes at home. Van Dyke also recorded many more women in factory work: "Eighty per cent of 1968's light industry training . . . [was] reserved for women."[22] Women on the farms had expanded roles too. Apart from the work they had always done in agriculture, such as planting, caring for animals, harvesting, and preparing food, they now did jobs involving the heaviest labor handled before by the men who had left for the front lines, such as plowing, building

dikes, and digging canals. They even made bomb craters into fish ponds to improve the food supply.

The North Vietnamese mobilized virtually everyone for the war effort. Women all over North Vietnam took on extra duties during and immediately after air raids, then went back to their usual work as soon as they could. Even women whose injuries or illness forced them out of military service found a way to contribute at home. Nguyen Thuy Mau's experience was not unusual. "My health was such a problem that I was sent back to the rear [away from combat]. But there was no place for me. My boyfriend had married someone else and I was too sick to find another man. . . . So I went for awhile to live in an all-women's collective farm with other women who had no place to go."[23]

Women also began to take positions of responsibility in the government. Van Dyke notes: "At the beginning of 1967, there were four female [vice-chairpersons in government departments], and women held 15 per cent of the seats in the National Assembly."[24] This reflected that the status of women in North Vietnam had permanently changed, and that there could be no return to their previous second-class status even after the war was over.

Chapter 2:
Medical Personnel and Welfare Workers in Vietnam

❧

The Vietnam War generated a horrendous number of injuries and illnesses, both from combat wounds and from other causes. Women treated the injured, both military and civilian. The war was also a disruptive force throughout Vietnam. Children became orphans and others were separated from their parents due to military service or other critical war work. In all these areas, women found roles to give aid to others.

"Sometimes There Was No Anesthesia and the Men Screamed"

North Vietnamese Army and Viet Cong medical personnel were mostly women. Women were considered to be more adept as healers, perhaps because this was in accord with their traditional role within the family. Further, women caregivers were seen as more comforting to the injured. Whatever the perceptions, women did perform effectively in this role.

Though not combat soldiers, women medical personnel faced many of the same problems as frontline troops. Kim

Cuc, a young woman who trained as a pediatrician, enlisted in the North Vietnamese Army (NVA) in 1965 and was soon in charge of a field hospital unit, where she commanded fifty other women and seven men. Kim Cuc's unit labored under conditions typical of the difficulties facing the entire NVA. Poor transportation and the ever-present threat of aerial attack hampered them at all times. Kim Cuc recalled,

> We traveled for three months on foot, carrying our supplies. [After] the first five days, I felt I couldn't go on. . . . I couldn't eat anything. But I had to march at the end of the group, because I was a doctor, and could help anyone who got sick and fell behind. . . . After the seventh day, my spirits came back. [Once they were at the front,] there were . . . [enemy] helicopters that could travel anywhere and spot people. We had to disguise the hospital.[25]

The hospital unit was always prepared to move on a moment's notice, yet the women had to treat the wounded and sick even as they relocated. This was especially harrowing as nurses ran the risk of being captured or killed by enemy troops or killed in an air attack.

Like the rest of the army, the hospital unit had to make do with minimal supplies in a hostile environment. Rice was sometimes in such short supply that it was reserved for patients; the hospital staff had to eat leaves from the forest. Nurses spent a lot of time foraging for food, and some were lost without a trace. Historian Albert Marrin recounts some of the perils they faced in the jungle: "Stampeding elephants [crushed workers], . . . tigers [and other animals preyed on people] . . . [but] the smaller creatures were the worst. Poisonous snakes bit scores of [people] . . . Some places were infested by leeches [or malaria-carrying mosquitoes]."[26] Medical supplies were scarce too. Kim Cuc recalled, "Sometimes there was no anesthesia [for surgery] and the men screamed."[27]

Although Kim Cuc had finished a regular course of study for medicine at Hanoi Medical College, she had no clinical experience before she went in the field, and at times had to pull out an anatomy book to determine how to treat a patient. Other women who served were even less prepared. Some female physicians had only a few years of elementary school education before get-

Most medical personnel in Vietnam were women. Here, a South Vietnamese nurse checks the vital signs of an emaciated prisoner of war.

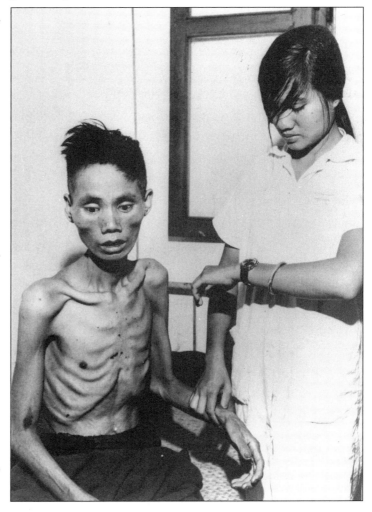

ting two years of medical training and going into the field. Nurses were similarly rushed into service. By North Vietnamese accounts, these women were still effective in treating casualties. Their compassion and motivation helped make up for their inexperience. Eventually, those who survived the war gained the experience they needed. Kim Cuc, for example, spent ten years on the front lines as a doctor.

Medical Workers of the U.S. Military

Nurses were the largest group of women out of approximately fifteen thousand American women in Vietnam during the war. The only American women serving in the medical field in South Vietnam were nurses, and most nurses were women. Women doctors did not serve with the U.S. forces at this time.

Women medical personnel of the Western allies operated under very different conditions from those of the North Vietnamese and Viet Cong. Most worked at bases that were far from combat, and they were supplied with everything necessary to care for the injured and sick. In most cases, severely wounded patients were delivered to army hospitals directly from the front lines by helicopter. A few nurses were closer to combat areas, but still in secure bases.

The presence of female nurses in the army reflected the opportunities available to women in America. American women had few intellectually challenging career choices as the 1960s began. Those who did not get married after graduating from high school could usually only become either teachers, secretaries, or nurses. Most other jobs open to women were relatively unskilled; the few really glamorous occupations, like stewardess, journalist, and actress, were hard jobs to get. A few women were doctors, lawyers, or worked in other professions, but these were exceptional for their time. They did not stand as examples of real career options for most women. It is not surprising, then, that many women went into nursing during this time.

Nurses in American military service completed nursing school before they joined the American armed services. Some had worked in civilian jobs before they entered the service. Sharon Lane became a registered nurse and worked for two years at a community hospital in Ohio. She enlisted in the army in April 1968, hoping for more interesting nursing work. Jill Ann Mishkel followed a similar path; she enlisted in 1969 because, as she said, "Basically, I was bored. I finally decided that if there was a war going on and even though I was so much against it, . . . I could go over there

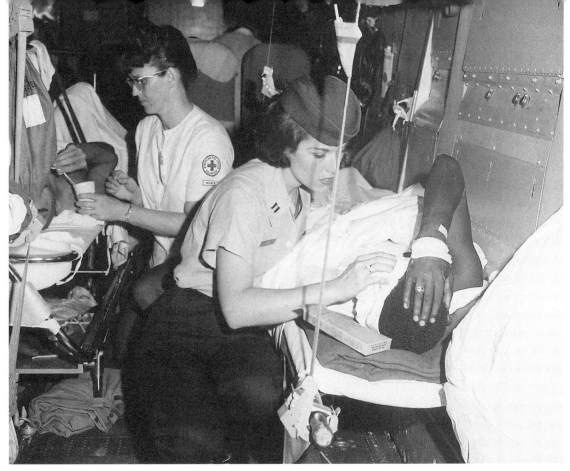

The majority of the American women who served in Vietnam were nurses. The armed forces did not allow women to serve in combat or as doctors.

and do something useful."[28]

Other nurses had more experience. Rose Sandecki, for example, had worked for seven years and had a bachelor's degree (most nurses had only completed high school and nursing school). Because of her experience, she joined the army as a captain; most nurses started out as second lieutenants, a lower military rank. With the increased rank came increased responsibility. Sandecki's first assignment in Vietnam was to be the head nurse of an intensive care unit (ICU), even though she had never worked in an ICU while a civilian.

"I Don't Know How We Did It"

Captain Sandecki's assignment typified one aspect of the job for army nurses in South Vietnam. They were given much more responsibility for their rank and experience than were civilian nurses in the United States or even military nurses outside the war zone. This was due to a shortage of nurses and to the way the

Sharon Lane

❦

Twenty-five-year-old First Lieutenant Sharon A. Lane, an army nurse, was killed by a Viet Cong rocket on the morning of June 8, 1969. She had been in Vietnam for six weeks.

Lane grew up in Canton, Ohio, and graduated from high school in 1961. She graduated from nursing school at Canton's Aultman Hospital in 1965 and went to work there as a maternity nurse. After two years she quit. She wanted a more dynamic career than a community hospital could offer. She enlisted in the U.S. Army Nurse Corps on April 18, 1968.

Lane arrived at the 312th Evacuation Hospital at Chu Lai, South Vietnam, on April 29, 1969. She started in the ICU (intensive care unit). Lane arrived just as fighting intensified; she was very busy from the start. Philip Bigler, in his biog-raphy *Hostile Fire: The Life and Death of First Lieutenant Sharon Lane*, quotes her as feeling needed and welcomed. "Would you believe that I like it here better than [Colorado]? Here everyone needs all the help . . . he can get, so it is much more warm and open." The hours were long, hard, and often hectic.

After two weeks, Lane was reassigned to the Vietnamese ward. She usually had overnight duty. Although the ward was understaffed, she enjoyed the work. She still worked in the ICU once a week.

Before sunrise on June 8, Viet Cong launched two small rockets at the Chu Lai base complex. One of these unaimed rockets landed on the Vietnamese ward where Sharon Lane was on duty. A single piece of shrapnel (a metal fragment) hit her, killing her instantly.

army hospitals were structured in South Vietnam.

The army maintained three types of facilities: Mobile Army Surgical Hospitals (popularly known as MASH units), evacuation hospitals, and convalescent hospitals. MASH units were small hospitals intended primarily for treatment of combat casualties. They were near what is known as "the front," an area where combat is expected at any time.

Evacuation hospitals were much bigger units on large U.S. bases; these handled both surgical (wounds) and medical (disease-related) cases. Convalescent hospitals were limited to treatment of patients whose problems were minor but required a period of recovery, such as simple fractures or recuperation from malaria.

The MASH units were intended to handle a sudden influx of seriously injured patients delivered by rescue helicopter. There were often more patients to be treated than the doctors could handle. Therefore, the nurses gave treatment as necessary. Nurses performed procedures normally done by a doctor because in this setting, there usually was not time to wait for a doctor. Nurses administered pain-killing drugs, debrided wounds (this involved the cleaning of the wound and the removal of destroyed flesh), and did emergency procedures such as tracheotomies (cutting a hole into the patient's windpipe through the front of the neck to bypass breathing blockages). They also assisted doctors on more involved surgeries, though most nurses had little or no surgical experience prior to coming into the army.

The evacuation hospitals also handled casualties directly off the battlefield, since MASH units were not always located close to a battle and had limited capacity. Nurses in the receiving and emergency departments of evacuation hospitals were usually responsible for triage. Triage was the practice of separating incoming patients into three categories. The "expectants" were patients who were unlikely to survive even if treated at once. The "walking wounded" were in no danger from their injuries, and

could wait for treatment. The remaining patients, called the "immediates," got first priority, as they had life-threatening wounds but with treatment might survive. The expectants went to a ward where they were monitored for signs that they might recover, in which case they were treated immediately. One unusual problem nurses faced is that many of the injured still had their weapons; nurses often had to calm down hysterical soldiers and coax their weapons away

A nurse changes a patient's dressing at an evacuation hospital. Located on U.S. bases, evacuation hospitals handled surgical and medical cases.

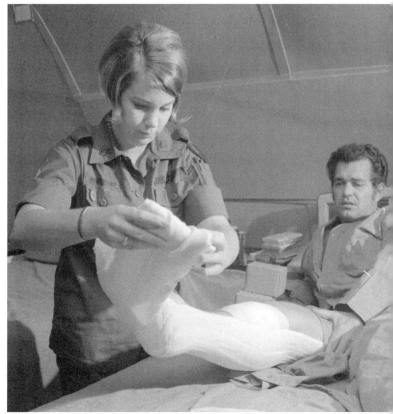

from them so they could be treated. Once those with urgent problems were stabilized and moved either to ICU or one of the other wards, the medical staff turned their attention to the walking wounded.

As there were few doctors, and they spent little time in the wards, all other care fell mostly to the nurses and corpsmen. Army nurses typically worked twelve-hour shifts, six days a week. The work was exhausting, and shifts were not always limited to twelve hours; Army nurse Jane Piper recalled, "[We worked] from seven [at night] to seven [in the morning]. We'd sit at [a staff meeting at the end of shift] and pass around these huge juice cans. We'd be so dehydrated that we'd go through four cans during [the meeting]. . . . [Then, depending on how busy we were,] we'd decide who got to go back to bed first."[29] Sometimes

American nurses at a hospital in Saigon visit with a wounded marine. Nurses typically worked exhausting twelve-hour shifts with few days off.

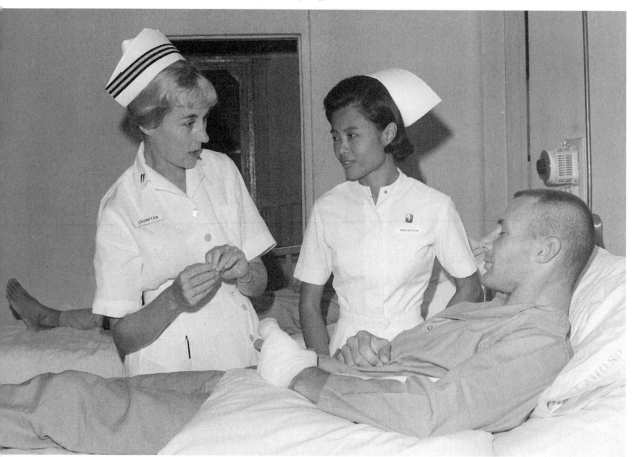

Women of the Vietnam War

the nurses worked even harder. Army nurse Charlotte Capozoli Miller remembered, "We worked [these very long hours] sometimes for twelve to fifteen days in a row if staff was short. . . . I don't know how we did it."[30]

The U.S. Navy also had nurses in Vietnam, intended to treat injured U.S. Marines. Twenty served in a station hospital in Saigon from the beginning of 1965 to April 1966, and ninety-five more served at the station hospital at Da Nang from November 1966 to June 1970. These station hospitals functioned in the same manner as the army evacuation hospitals, and were supported by offshore hospital ships with many more nurses serving aboard.

Australian Military Nurses

Altogether there were 460 Australian medical personnel serving in South Vietnam during the war, including doctors, nurses, X-ray technicians, and other support personnel. Most of the women in this group were nurses, but there was at least one female X-ray technician. The Australian medical personnel were there primarily to support Australian troops that assisted the Americans and the ARVN in the fight against the Communists, but they also treated many Vietnamese civilians.

At first, Australian nurses had to cope with a shortage of supplies, since the Australian government did not know how to support hospitals in a war zone. The hospitals were short of the most basic supplies and equipment on a chronic basis, until they began to seek help with supplies from the Americans. This worked very well; Australian medical units were soon some of the most efficient in South Vietnam. As in the American hospitals, the nurses bore a heavy burden in sustaining these operations, working twelve-hour shifts, six days a week. In a crisis, they worked even more. The Tet Offensive (a series of intense battles during the Vietnamese lunar new year festival on January 31, 1968) was the biggest crisis, as the Communists made all-out attacks across South Vietnam. The Australian nurses worked for thirty-six hours straight to treat all the injuries.

The Australian nurses triaged patients differently than the Americans. The most severely injured soldiers were treated first, no matter their chance of survival. Because of this, and a faster processing procedure for patients than the U.S. Army had, the Australians managed to save the lives of 97.4 percent of their wounded patients. This was an incredible success rate, especially compared to the very commendable American casualty survival rate of about 95 percent.

Just like the Americans, the Australian nurses were not psychologically prepared for the severity and volume of injuries when they first got to South Vietnam. Nurse Anne Healy, who worked in the ICU at Vung Tau, said, "Anyone who works in a casualty [ward back home] sees horrendous things. [Auto] accidents are not nice, injuries at the wharves and things are multiple traumas. But [Vietnam] was multiple trauma on a grand scale."[31]

Civilian Hospitals in South Vietnam

Vietnamese and Western nurses, almost always women, staffed a variety of civilian treatment facilities in South Vietnam. In some cases Vietnamese nurses received training from Western nurses. A few South Vietnamese women doctors also worked in civilian hospitals.

South Vietnam had a shortage of doctors and nurses before the war, and the few hospitals that existed were poorly equipped for the most part. When the war started, both Australian and American military nurses helped train South Vietnamese women as nurses. Female Vietnamese health care workers were also employed at hospitals set up by Western organizations.

One such hospital was the National Center for Plastic and Reconstructive Surgery in Saigon. It was sponsored by the New York–based Children's Medical Relief International with the intention of providing treatment for children injured by the war. Among its doctors was Dr. My (her full name is not known), one of the few women doctors in South Vietnam. Dr. My was on duty when a nine-year-old girl named Phan Thi Kim Phuc was brought to the hospital. She had been horribly burned in an air attack. Against all the normal admission rules of the hospital, Dr. My insisted that the girl be treated immediately, and in so doing, certainly saved Kim Phuc's life. Credit must also go to a nurse, Lien Huong, who sought out the doctor to see the girl. This compassionate response by these two women was in the best tradition of the medical professions.

Combat and Casualties Among Medical Providers

Despite attempts to isolate them from battle, nurses faced plenty of risks during the war. Historian Philip Bigler notes that American nurses first suffered injuries in December 1964: "Four U. S. Navy nurses were wounded in a . . . terrorist bombing . . . in downtown Saigon. . . . All . . . performed heroically in tending to the other casualties."[32] In total, eight American female military nurses died in South Vietnam during the war. Of these, five were killed in aircraft accidents unrelated to combat and two died of medical problems

The Girl in the Picture

Phan Thi Kim Phuc was born April 6, 1963, to Phan Tung and his wife, Nu, in a hamlet northeast of Saigon. The Phans were peasants who ran a small restaurant.

From the age of seven, Kim Phuc (the name means "golden happiness") helped at the family restaurant and went to school. She was in the second grade when the war first touched her life; as Denise Chong describes in *The Girl in the Picture*, Kim Phuc's brother burst into her classroom. "Brother-in-law is dead!" he shouted. Her uncle, a South Vietnamese soldier, had been killed by the Viet Cong. From that time, the Viet Cong became more active in the area where the Phans lived.

Kim Phuc's life changed forever on June 8, 1972. Viet Cong soldiers took over the Phan house to confront the South Vietnamese army. The family took refuge in a temple for two days, but as the fighting intensified, they fled again, with many others, down a road. A South Vietnamese bomber mistook the fleeing people for Viet Cong and dropped napalm, a fire bomb. Napalm splashed onto Kim Phuc, setting her on fire. A journalist took a picture of the nine-year-old as she ran toward him, screaming in pain and terror.

The picture, widely published around the world, came to symbolize the horror of modern war. Kim Phuc survived, despite severe burns. She spent over a year in the hospital before finally returning to her family. Kim Phuc still has trouble with her injuries, but she has been able to live normally for the most part. She eventually sought political asylum in Canada, where she continues to live with her husband and two sons.

This photo of Phan Thi Kim Phuc running naked from her burning village became a symbol of the horror of modern war.

These nurses received Purple Heart medals for their bravery during a terrorist bombing in Saigon. Nurses often faced extremely dangerous situations.

unrelated to combat. First Lieutenant Sharon Lane, an army nurse, was killed by a Viet Cong rocket attack on the evacuation hospital at which she was on duty in 1966. She was the only American woman to be killed in combat in Vietnam while in the military. Other nurses were injured on occasion, either through noncombat mishaps, or as a consequence of attacks.

At least one civilian nurse, a missionary nurse named Betty Olsen, also died in Vietnam. She helped Vietnamese suffering from leprosy, a disfiguring dis-

ease. She was captured by North Vietnamese troops during the Tet Offensive. While in captivity, she helped another captive American, Mike Benge, survive a severe case of malaria. Some weeks later she got sick and died. Benge recalled, "It took her about a week to die. . . . I begged [the North Vietnamese] to bring water so I could wash her, but [they would not]. They just let her lie there."[33]

Nurses who cared for prisoners of war (POWs) also had to be careful. Many POWs were too badly injured to threaten anyone, and others behaved well, but some did not. U.S. Navy nurse Maureen Walsh recalled one Viet Cong POW: "I brought dinner to [a POW who] was in a bed with two casts on her legs. . . . I gave the woman a tray and turned around to get a sheet, and she had picked up a fork and was going [for] my back. I just turned around in time and knocked it out of her hand."[34]

No Australian nurses in Vietnam died during the war. Their hospital at the village of Baria was attacked twice by Viet Cong in 1969, but both times no one was injured. They also faced other risks. In one case, Australian nurse Jan Mills was conducting a health care inspection in a village. She and her guides ran into a Viet Cong soldier, who demanded they leave. Mills said, "[My visit] was obviously ill-timed, but apart from the initial shock, nothing really major occurred."[35] The point of the health inspections was to help Vietnamese families by reviewing practices relating to sanitation and safety. It is ironic that this program, designed to reduce health risks for Vietnamese women and children, could put an Australian nurse at risk.

Child Care

Many women also played a role in child care during the Vietnam War. Before the war, child care in Vietnam was primarily the responsibility of the mother by tradi-tion, or in her absence, her extended family. However, many North Vietnamese women were unable to care for their own children because of their war obligations. Other Vietnamese women were killed in the war or involuntarily separated from their children, and some South Vietnamese women abandoned children who were fathered by Americans. Children in

Many children were orphaned during the war after being involuntarily separated from their mothers.

need of care went to child care facilities and orphanages, which were staffed primarily by women.

North Vietnamese child care facilities were supported by the Hanoi government. Child care centers staffed by women were established in cities near factories so that women could take jobs in industry. The government recognized the importance of these centers by publicizing the efforts of the caregivers. For example, Nguyen Thi Thao was recognized for her efforts as a child care worker in Hanoi during the air attacks there. Child care in the larger collective farms was handled by women staffing a nursery; children usually started in the nursery at the age of six months so their mothers could go back to the fields. On smaller farms the arrangements were less formal, with women sharing babysitting duties.

South Vietnam had no equivalent to the system in the north for child care. If a mother died because of the war, and the remaining family could not care for the child, the only other choice was a private orphanage, where the caregivers were typically women. Many single or widowed mothers abandoned one or more children to orphanages because they had no hope of feeding them. Unfortunately for the orphans, many of the orphanages were run for profit; the proprietors took government subsidies but as they were paid based on the number of children in their facility, not the condition of the children, they spent the absolute minimum amount to keep the children alive. The Vietnamese women who worked as caregivers thus had far too many children to care for, too little food for the children, and next to no training. Conditions were horrible, with up to 80 percent of the children dying each year in some orphanages.

The best of the orphanages were those run by Roman Catholic and Buddhist nuns. Motivated not by profit, but by their faith, they offered a higher level of care, because their aim was to do their best for the children, not to make money. They cared for children directly, and also concentrated on getting charitable aid for their charges. Most significantly for the welfare of the orphans, the nuns did whatever they could to facilitate adoption.

Adoption

Some of the nuns directing orphanages were effective in arranging adoptions despite the difficulties caused by the South Vietnamese government bureaucracy. Most adoptions were to Westerners, and the government required a lot of paperwork to authorize a foreign adoption. Reporter Ann Bryan Mariano recalls one orphanage run by a Viet-

Amerasians

❧

Amerasian children were the products of intimate relationships between Vietnamese women and American men. Thousands of Amerasian children were born in South Vietnam by the end of the war. Some immigrated to the United States with one or both parents, but most remained in Vietnam. Among those remaining, the luckier ones had a mother or other family members who raised them, but many were abandoned to orphanages.

Orphans were the forgotten children of South Vietnam. Many Vietnamese thought adoption risked adding bad blood to the family. This was especially true of Amerasian children, whom Vietnamese referred to as *bui doi*—children of the dust. During the war almost all of the adoptions, particularly of Amerasian children, were foreign adoptions, with most of these children going to America and Australia. While this guaranteed much better prospects for the health and education of the children, some of them grew to feel alienated from their origins as Vietnamese. On the other hand, these adoptees were lucky; many children in Vietnamese orphanages died before they grew up, so miserable were the conditions there.

Those Amerasians who reached adulthood in Vietnam had the lowest status in society. They were racially mixed, which most Vietnamese considered to be a mark of inherent inferiority, and their existence was also a constant reminder of the former American presence. Because of their low status they could not get a good education or a good job. Many continue to live in Vietnam today, while others have been able to immigrate to the United States.

namese Roman Catholic sister, Sister Robert Tron: "She had an irrepressible spirit. . . . Her mission was simple. Get as many children out of Vietnam as possible."[36] This was especially important with regard to mixed-race orphans, who were looked down upon by most Vietnamese. Sister Tron helped organize dozens of adoptions of children, many of them racially mixed, to families in America. In 1970 there were an estimated twenty thousand orphans in South Vietnam, but less than two thousand were formally adopted during that year, almost all by overseas parents. Sister Tron managed to arrange several dozen overseas adoptions that year, an example of the efforts made by nuns on behalf of orphans.

Western women also worked hard to find homes for Vietnamese orphans. Sue

Timmins and Rosemary Taylor, two Australian women, were two of the most effective. Timmins volunteered her time at a large orphanage in Saigon, and soon began working with Taylor, a volunteer with the World Council of Churches, to arrange adoptions. Taylor spent eight years in South Vietnam, during which time she managed to place about eight thousand adoptees.

There was some controversy about whether it was right to remove children from their home country and send them to adoptive families in Western countries with very different cultures. On the one hand, Vietnamese children who went to America or other affluent nations as adoptees would get far better nutrition, far better medical care, and a far better education than if they stayed in Vietnam. They would also be removed from their home culture and language, though, and might never have a chance to be truly Vietnamese. Rosemary Taylor had no regrets about her part in arranging foreign adoptions:

Surely, let a child grow up with his biological parents in his own country, if the option exists. But for abandoned children, such an option does not exist. . . . The culture of the Asian orphanage . . . may consist of disease, discomfort, [little or no education], and a despair and feeling of worthlessness. . . . What makes anyone so smugly sure that these children would not profit from parental love and support; from a healthy diet; from adequate medical care; and from good education opportunities?[37]

As with any activity in Vietnam, there were risks for women who assisted in the adoption of orphans. Some of the risk was incidental to simply being in Vietnam, with the constant and unpredictable combat. Ironically, though, the only recorded deaths of Western women involved in adoption work had nothing to do with combat. A U.S. Air Force jet evacuating orphans from South Vietnam crashed due to mechanical fault in April 1975, killing two Australian women caregivers, Lee Makk and Margaret Moses, along with three female American Red Cross workers, a U.S. Army nurse, and many orphans.

Charitable Agencies and Missionaries

While some foreign women worked to find homes outside of Vietnam for orphans, others wanted to provide aid to the people in South Vietnam. Most were volunteers for private charitable agencies, often with religious affiliations.

About thirty women served as volunteers in Vietnam under the auspices of the American Friends Service Committee between 1966 and 1975. This was a volunteer Quaker relief group which was in South Vietnam to help civilians deal with injuries suffered in the war. They established a rehabilitation center for this purpose in Quang Ngai Province. The women volunteers taught Vietnamese to staff the center, training them in the fields of physical therapy, prosthetics, and nursing, so the center would sustain itself after the volunteers left. One of the volunteers, physical therapist Dot Weiler, wrote about the volunteers' dedication to their mission: "We were absolutely neutral in regards to the political situation and vowed to treat anyone who came to our center as long as they were civilians."[38] When the last volunteers left about six months after the fall of Saigon, the rehabilitation center was staffed by trained Vietnamese who were able to keep providing services to their countrymen. This proved to be a lasting legacy of the efforts of these women.

An American woman poses with her adopted Vietnamese daughter. Many Vietnamese orphans were sent to live with American families.

Other women worked for charitable institutions such as International Voluntary Services (IVS) and Catholic Relief Services. IVS concentrated on community development projects, such as working to rehabilitate Vietnamese juvenile delinquents (usually homeless boys), assisting nuns in establishing orphanages, improving adult literacy, or helping youth groups work to assist refugees. Sandra Collingwood was one of the IVS volunteers in South Vietnam, beginning in 1967. She lived with Vietnamese families during part of this time, in order to better understand their way of life, and thus be more effective in helping them.

Western women who worked alone with the Vietnamese, as did most IVS volunteers, faced unique problems. For one thing, they suffered frequent verbal sexual harassment from American troops. This unwanted attention usually occurred when American troops were moving through the community where the women volunteers were working. The woman volunteer was embarrassed for being treated as if she were a prostitute, and it caused embarrassment to the Vietnamese she worked with as well, who respected the volunteers like village elders. Another problem IVS women volunteers faced was that IVS supervisors were unwilling to allow a woman to go by herself to projects that were isolated from American military forces because they feared for the safety of a woman in that situation. The same limitations were not placed on male volunteers.

On the whole, women in nursing and welfare roles had their share of frustrations, working against a system and a situation geared to war rather than the well-being of everyday people. It is remarkable they accomplished as much as they did.

Chapter 3:
Keeping Spirits Up

During the Vietnam War, Western troops were far from home, in a place where everything was unfamiliar and uncomfortable—from the weather to the living conditions to the attitudes of the Vietnamese. Some troops were volunteers, but most had been drafted into the war and had to serve a year in Vietnam before they could rotate out. For all these reasons, the morale of the troops was a major concern, and the American government therefore went to great lengths to keep the spirits of the troops up. Women figured heavily in the staffing of American support services, which included putting on live shows for troops all over Vietnam, creating stores and shops to offer luxury items and services to Americans, and providing other forms of diversion, from recreation centers to special radio shows to short visits at the front by Red Cross volunteers. Women entertainers were especially valuable in helping to keep troops motivated, and to remind troops of the more enjoyable aspects of life, in contrast to the gloom of war.

The PX System

Women worked in various roles in the post exchange (PX) system in Vietnam, also known as the Vietnam Regional Exchange. This was a network of U.S. government–run stores providing health and morale items to American servicemen and their allies. PX services were supposed to help make life in the war zone more bearable by offering the comforts and conveniences of home. Soldiers could order everything from pizzas to refrigerators to diamond rings to silverware. They were also able to buy and sell stocks through brokers and order automobiles for delivery in the United States. The largest volume of goods sold included snacks, reading material, toothpaste, and other day-to-day sundries that normally were not available in Vietnam.

A large proportion of the sales clerks and secretaries at the PX outlets were English-speaking women. Recruiters found it difficult to interest many American women in filling these jobs in Vietnam, though. They turned to women in

A South Vietnamese woman sells stolen PX items. Many goods stolen from the PX were sold on Vietnam's thriving black market.

other countries and were able to recruit Australians, Filipinas, New Zealanders, and Canadians, among others.

Women employed in the PX system worked in facilities ranging in size from department stores to fast-food stands. PX stores, snack stands, gift shops, barbershops, and other outlets were set up on practically every secure American base. Altogether there were about 300 stores and 150 food outlets in South Vietnam. Women cooked and served food, cut hair, sold goods, and incidentally also gave troops an opportunity to interact with English-speaking women. Other women did office work in support of PX operations.

PX jobs had their downside for the women who worked there. PX goods and services were available to Americans in South Vietnam, whether civilians or in the military, but, ironically, not for the English-speaking women from other countries who actually worked for the PX. Third-country nationals (employees who were neither American nor Vietnamese) were only allowed to purchase soft drinks, tobacco, and a few other items. They also suffered from unfair salary policies; women were paid less than men in the same job, Australians were paid less than Americans, and Filipinos were paid the least of all. Further, sixty-six-hour workweeks with shifts as long as twelve hours were not unusual.

Women working for the PX were also expected to live on the local economy. They had to find their own housing and buy food from Vietnamese sources. Fortunately, they were all paid very well by Vietnamese standards, so it was not difficult to make ends meet, though the goods available were of uneven quality. Ironically, many of the things PX workers bought were from the black market, in some cases items stolen from the PX.

Most PX jobs for women involved sales clerking or secretarial work. In many ways these jobs would have seemed indistinguishable from a job in America, since the work was inside, often in air-conditioned buildings, and nobody wore uniforms. The typist jobs could be especially tedious, because the army, with overall responsibility for the PX system, had a policy of not accepting any typographical errors in its documents. This was before the time of computer word processors or photocopy machines; any error either had to be corrected on multiple carbon copies, or the page had to be completely retyped.

The PX did have a few more interesting jobs for women. Helen Keayes, for example, became an information specialist for the PX system. Her job was to promote the operations of the PX system in Vietnam on local radio and television, and through PX-issued newspapers. She did promotional articles illustrated with smiling staffers, extolled the excellent service, and detailed special offers available each week. She developed a knack for folksy prose in her articles that impressed her superiors. For example, to accompany a photo of the opening of a new snack bar, she wrote, "Snack time for the military police at the Long Binh Porta-Kamp Snack Bar. The shady annex makes every meal a picnic."[39] These features helped distract soldiers from the dreariness of war, and helped improve morale.

Entertainment for the North Vietnamese

Both sides in the war tried to provide diversions to their troops in the field to improve morale. One of the most effective ways was to bring professional entertainers to the troops near the front. Women were essential members of these entertainment troupes.

While the North Vietnamese recognized the value of entertainment as a morale booster to their soldiers, they had a hard time providing this because

Helen Keayes

Australian Helen Keayes was one of the most outrageous women to go to Vietnam during the war. She was hired by the U. S. Department of Defense to work as a clerk-typist for the PX in South Vietnam in 1968. She later became a PX information specialist, which allowed her great leeway in traveling around South Vietnam.

Keayes had a blanket travel authorization so she could write stories and get photographs to promote the PX. She considered this a recreational opportunity. To do her work, she was issued an armored personnel carrier (a small armored vehicle with no guns). She learned to drive it, though she crushed some tents in the process. She also drafted written orders for air transport to anywhere in South Vietnam she wanted to go. While much of her travel was related to doing her job, many trips were simply a way to get to parties. Sometimes her orders were signed by real officers; sometimes she forged the signature of an officer who did not exist. She was never caught.

The pilots got to know Keayes and taught her how to fly helicopters. Later, she took friends for joyrides. She even landed a helicopter on the roof of allied headquarters once. This was not her most amazing escapade, though. She wanted to ride in a combat jet. Although it was not allowed, she claimed she arranged to be smuggled aboard a Phantom fighter in the navigator's seat. The pilot took her on a bombing mission over Hanoi. There is no independent verification that this happened, but if it did, Helen Keayes was the only woman to fly a combat mission over North Vietnam.

of transportation difficulties. Entertainers, always a mixed group of women and men, had to get to the troops the same way the troops got to the front—mostly on foot. They were unable to bring extensive costumes or other props, and adapted their dramatic presentations and songs to take this into account. They emphasized the roles of women in the types of productions they put on. All of the plays, for example, had prominent roles for women, and often included singing parts for women. The subject matter of these performances usually centered on simple or familiar themes. Former Viet Cong member Truong Nhu Tang recalled that they were about "guerrilla warfare, revolutionary heroes, [traditional tales], but they were always welcomed enthusiastically for the relief they provided from a rigorous and danger-filled routine."[40]

Women also were important as entertainers on the home front, both on stage and in movies. Actress Duc Hoan even took part in both film and stage productions. Regarding the showing of her work in an area of North Vietnam subjected to many American air raids, she said, "People had to have a life when they emerged from the bomb shelters. The government spent money on good props and cosmetics to cheer them. The government knew the value of films then."[41]

The USO and American Troops

The United Services Organization (USO) was active in providing both everyday recreational opportunities and special entertainment productions for soldiers in Vietnam. At its peak, the USO operated seventeen centers all over South Vietnam, managed mainly by American women. The USO women helped provide everyday comforts during the soldiers' leisure time. The first center was opened in Saigon in 1963. All were closed in June 1972, as American troops withdrew.

USO centers varied in size and composition. Maureen Nerli was an associate director of the club at Tan Son Nhut, the largest airport in South Vietnam. Her description of the club gives a good idea of what the others were like.

Not all USO centers were this big, but all were similarly equipped:

> It was . . . a four-story building. . . . We had pool and Ping-Pong tables, overseas telephones, a barber shop, and gift shop. We served between five hundred and eight hundred [milkshakes], hot dogs, and hamburgers every day. We had fifty Vietnamese on our staff, three assigned GIs, one . . . program assistant, one director, and three associate directors. The GIs came from all over— Tan Son Nhut, Long Binh, Da Nang—you name it.[42]

Apart from day-to-day operations at the clubs, the USO also had special events at the centers. For example, the women at one center put on an Oktoberfest with German food and other cultural touches. Some of the other events celebrated Mexican and Irish heritages, and that of the southern United States. Special events also centered around holidays, especially during the Christmas season. In every case, the women sought to remind the soldiers of the good things in life at home by bringing some of it to the men.

USO work was not confined to the centers. Women staffers would arrange to drive or fly into remote fire bases to provide entertainment and other services to the troops. Some of the USO women had backgrounds themselves as performers, so they might sing popular songs. During the Christmas season, they might lead the men in Christmas carols, or distribute small presents. They would often bring in a rock band that the USO had booked into the country, or other celebrities. The USO women would also bring food that was more interesting than the C rations the men on the front lines usually had to eat. Ice cream was especially popular, though in Vietnam's hot climate, it had to be brought in by helicopter and eaten quickly. Sometimes the women just talked to the soldiers; most of the troops appreciated talking to a woman, even for a few minutes, as a distraction from their dreary existence.

Visiting Entertainers

The USO might be best known for the celebrity entertainers it brought to South Vietnam. About half of these entertainers were women. These celebrities came over as volunteers, receiving no pay. Other types of performers were also brought into Vietnam; a high proportion of these were women. These performers differed from the volunteer celebrities in that they were paid for their efforts.

Many top-name celebrity women volunteered to do tours of Vietnam to boost the morale of American troops.

Some came on their own, such as comic Martha Raye. Others came over as part of one of the Bob Hope tours. Hope, a comedian, was the most celebrated entertainer of the war; he came to Vietnam during the Christmas season from 1964 through 1972. Each time, he brought other entertainers with him. Among the women associated with the Hope tours were singers and actresses Joey Heatherton, Anita Bryant, Anna Maria Alberghetti, Carroll Baker, Janis Paige, Ann-Margret, Connie Stevens, Raquel Welch, Jill St. John, Ursula Andress, and Lola Falana, as well as comedienne Phyllis Diller. Many of the women returned for multiple tours; singer Anita Bryant, for example, volunteered for three tours.

These female celebrities put on performances at large bases, small bases that were close to the fighting, and hospitals. These performances included skits, song-and-dance numbers, and a lot of jokes. The skits were always humorous and topical, relating to matters close to the soldiers' hearts, such as the absurdities of daily military life, or current events back home. Some of the song-and-dance artists, including Joey Heatherton and Nancy Sinatra, would get soldiers up on stage to sing and dance with them. The songs varied with the performer, but some women singers found that certain songs were requested again and again:

Ann-Margret was one of many female entertainers who came to Vietnam during the war with Bob Hope's Christmas tours.

"Proud Mary," "Something," "Leaving on a Jet Plane," "These Boots Were Made for Walking," and "We Gotta Get Out of This Place." Shows were generally closed with a patriotic song or a service-related one, such as "The Marine Hymn." Outside of the shows, some of the soldiers, including patients in hospital wards who were unable to attend performances, also got a chance to talk with the performers one-on-one.

As well known as the Bob Hope tours were, they represented a tiny fraction of the total USO entertainment effort. Altogether, the USO put on about fifty-six hundred performances in Vietnam. In fact, the USO provided more opportunities for performers than there were performers to fill them. Some very inexperienced performers, many of them women, thus had the opportunity to come to Vietnam. For example, Bobbi Jo Pettit was a member

Martha Raye

Martha Raye probably spent more time in South Vietnam than any other major American entertainer. For eight consecutive years, she spent several months at a time performing for troops and doing whatever else she could to raise morale. She had already had a long career as an actress, known for her unusual comedy and loud delivery. In fact, her nickname was "Old Big Mouth."

Martha Raye was born in 1916. She was a famous comedienne before World War II. She went to North Africa to entertain the troops in that war, but got sick in 1943 and had to return to the United States. As American troops became involved in Vietnam, she was among the first big-name performers to go there.

She went everywhere. No base was too dangerous, and the soldiers came to love her for this fearlessness. Raye did not escape unscathed, however. On two occasions, she was wounded by shrapnel. Frank Coffey, in *Always Home: Fifty Years of the USO—the Official Photographic History*, recorded her feelings about the injuries: "[It wasn't] so terrible. Just the ribs and a foot. I've had worse hangovers."

Raye visited patients in hospitals on a regular basis. She also was a fully qualified nurse. During her last tour in 1972 she was at an Army Special Forces base that was almost overrun by a Communist attack. She spent thirteen hours as a surgical nurse at the base's small hospital, refusing to go off duty until all the casualties were treated.

Martha Raye was given the honorary rank of lieutenant colonel in the Army Special Forces. The honor did not go to her head. Afterward, she referred to herself as "Colonel Big Mouth."

Actress Martha Raye performs a scene from Hello Dolly *for troops in Saigon in 1967.*

of an all-girl band, the Pretty Kittens, that went to Vietnam in May 1967. She related how their tour started: "Our first show was at the Saigon USO club. We would do from one to three shows a day, all different places. . . . It was ideal because we were the same age as most of the GIs, doing American songs that were very current right then."[43] The band members spent five months in Vietnam, constantly traveling by military truck or by helicopter, and they had to travel light. Apart from their guitars, they had a single suitcase each.

Performances on the road could be difficult for noncelebrity entertainers. Australian singer Jill Kennedy remarked, "We'd sleep on the cement at the airport waiting for a lift out to Da Nang or Pleiku or wherever. Australian so-called civilians were last on the list; [livestock] or anything would have first priority."[44] Kennedy was joking about the livestock, but otherwise was telling the truth; sometimes female performers had to wait days for transport.

Travel was complicated for some acts by the need to carry extensive costuming. This was particularly true for women who sang and danced, because their acts might call for multiple costume changes. Living arrangements on the road were also haphazard, and the facilities for dressing rooms were frequently nothing more than standard government issue (GI) tents. Sometimes the entertainers had a real stage on which to perform their acts, but in other cases they might be working on the back of a flatbed truck, or even a bare hilltop.

The paid female performers had to be approved by the Commercial Entertainment Auditioning Committee, a part of the U.S. Army. The committee would rate the show on appearance, quality, length, and costuming, paying as much as $420 for a single one-woman singing performance. In an era when a salary of $12,000 a year in the United States was considered very good, many performers could earn a net payoff of $1,000 or more per week. It is also notable that in this field, women seemed to be paid as well as men.

At the largest bases, the entertainers might put on the same basic show three times: once for officers, once for non-commissioned officers (higher-ranked enlisted personnel), and the last for regular enlisted men. In all cases, the women were very popular with their audiences. Most of the men already felt deprived of contact with women from home. It was exhilarating to be able to watch and listen to talented women doing their best to make the troops happy. There is no doubt the women knew this, and they made it a part of their act. For example, singer Frances

Raquel Welch dances with a group of soldiers in Da Nang. Female performers helped boost the morale of U.S. troops throughout the war.

Langford, who had entertained U.S. troops during World War II, told her Vietnam audience, "You had better like me! I played for your fathers."[45] The women too got joy from this relationship. Australian dancer Elizabeth Burton said, "All you had to do was walk on stage and they just screamed! You'll never get a better audience than a troop audience."[46]

Risks to Entertainers

While the Vietnam War held risks for everyone at all times, women entertain-

ers faced a particular set of perils. Part of this risk arose out of their need to travel extensively and to go to locations that were more exposed to the risks of combat. Other risks were tied directly to their nature as performers.

In order to reach their audiences, female performers were constantly flying in and out of combat zones and driving through a countryside that might include Viet Cong snipers. For that matter, enemy artillery attacks might hit a base during a performance. Some performers

Women of the Vietnam War

suffered minor injuries from such attacks, though the injuries were usually not the result of shells exploding, but instead from falls or other mishaps while scrambling to take cover. Indeed, even the famous were not immune to injury; actress Martha Raye was wounded twice by enemy fire and was awarded the Purple Heart, an American military medal issued for being wounded in combat.

Women performers could also be endangered by the very men they were there to entertain. Maureen Elkner's rock group, for example, came close to being hurt in the middle of a concert. They were performing on stage when a disgruntled soldier attacked his own commander with a hand grenade. The grenade exploded in the front rows of the audience and injured sixty-two people, but the singers escaped unscathed. One Australian woman, Cathy Warnes, was killed while performing as a singer, when a U.S. serviceman attempted to murder his commanding officer and shot her instead.

Women performers also faced the risk of unwanted sexual advances by soldiers. All of the women put up with some verbal sexual harassment, in an era when such comments by men were rarely condemned. Most of the risk was controlled by simple security measures, such as armed guards or secure nighttime quarters. The security precautions were not always effective to keep the women physically safe, however. At least two Australian performers were raped by American soldiers, and there were probably other rapes that went unreported.

Army Special Services

The USO, a private organization and not affiliated with the government, did not fill all the recreation needs of the American forces in South Vietnam. The U.S. Army Special Services office also provided entertainment for its troops in servicemen's clubs at locations not covered by the USO. These clubs, each run by just one or two women hired by Special Services, were typically simpler than USO clubs. One example, the club at Vinh Long airfield, had a kitchen, a lounge, a music room complete with a set of drums, and a library. A swimming pool was under construction but never completed.

As with the USO, the purpose of these clubs was to offer diversions to the men when they were off duty. Georgeanne Duffy Andreason worked at Vinh Long. She recalled the atmosphere of the club to be low-key: "We tried to plan as many activities as possible and to bring in any outside entertainment; however, the latter was infrequent. We found ourselves spending many hours in the lounge just listening to the men 'ventilate.'"[47] The men talked about their frustrations dealing with the ARVN troops, or about the number of times their aircraft had been hit by enemy bullets that day, and most often, tragic stories about buddies killed or wounded.

About four dozen women were working for Special Services in 1968. The activities and entertainment mirrored those that took place at USO clubs, although simpler, since USO clubs had many more people on staff. Because the Special Service clubs were in more isolated areas than USO clubs, they were a little less secure against Viet Cong attacks. Andreason, for example, had to be evacuated during the Tet Offensive, and the club sustained damage from Viet Cong mortar attacks.

Like USO women, women working for Special Services also went away from the clubs on occasion to serve the needs of smaller units. These visits were to deliver such things as magazines or special food packages, and of course to give the men a chance to take their minds off of their duties.

"Doughnut Dollies"

The American Red Cross (ARC) was another group predominantly staffed by women that worked to support troops in the field. ARC enlisted the help of hundreds of American women to implement its programs in South Vietnam. The women were often called "Doughnut Dollies," a term which was first used for their predecessors in World War II, who often handed out doughnuts and coffee. ARC women did not actually serve doughnuts in Vietnam, but they conducted a number of morale-supporting programs.

The doughnut dollies worked at ARC centers at twenty-eight bases in Vietnam. A typical club had facilities for volleyball, billiards, and shuffleboard, as well as a library. Two to eight women would staff each club. They would help soldiers write letters home; many of the troops were not able to write well, and others were not sure how to put their feelings into words. The doughnut dollies could also help arrange for short-term loans if the soldier needed money for leave before payday. This was an issue, because some of the men were careless with their money and would not have been able to enjoy their leave if broke.

The doughnut dollies also helped with other problems; for example, in at least one case, a doughnut dollie managed to talk a depressed soldier into following orders, where failure to do so might have resulted in severe discipline. Sometimes the women would just listen to lonely or upset soldiers who needed to talk to a sympathetic listener.

Off-duty men stationed at the large bases needed these services, but men on duty needed assistance too. To help these men, doughnut dollies often made visits directly to units in the field. They would be moved by helicopter from unit to unit, spending about an hour in each location. They would interact with five to twenty soldiers, playing simple games. The doughnut dollies prepared the game content ahead of time and created props to go along with the game. The idea was to involve the soldiers in an activity which would take their minds off the war and the dismal living conditions for a short time. One doughnut dollie, Jeanne Bokina Christie said, "In many cases the games were so silly that [the men would laugh]. Sometimes we would laugh so hard that they would laugh hard. It sounds a bit out of context, but it did the trick; it gave them a lift that was needed to survive."[48]

Occasionally, these women returned with the personal effects of an injured soldier who had been evacuated from that unit for medical treatment. They went to the hospital to give the wounded soldier his belongings. These doughnut dollies were not accustomed to

A Red Cross worker gives a care package to an injured officer. Staffed mostly by women, the American Red Cross provided a number of services to U.S. troops.

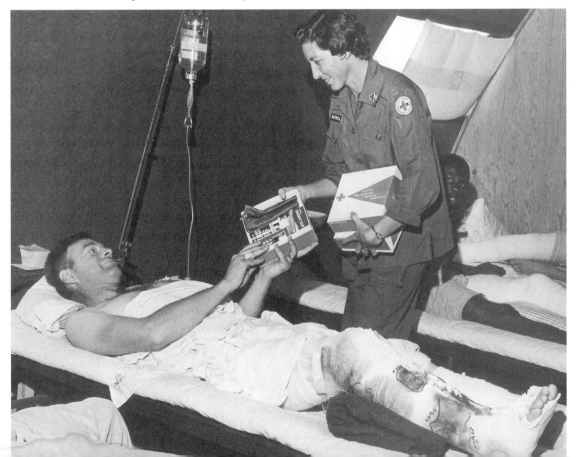

being around injured soldiers on a daily basis; some felt these trips were the toughest duty they faced.

Doughnut dollies had another somber duty: They were often the point of contact between a wounded soldier and his family. These women specialized in this role, spending all their working time in hospitals. They wrote health and welfare reports for many of the casualties in order to provide some real information to the GI's loved ones. They talked to the soldiers, if they could, to supplement medical information with more personal facts. If the patient could not talk, they would get information from the doctor treating the patient. In either case this report would be sent on to the family, explaining the soldier's condition and his probable recovery process.

Apart from reporting duties, doughnut dollies in the hospitals did what they could to help the casualties with nonmedical matters. In this regard, they were doing the same sorts of things that the doughnut dollies working with combat units did—helping men to write letters, for example. They were also there for the patients to talk to, though the women's reporting duties kept them very busy.

The various roles women accepted to give support to the men in the military varied widely, but they all had a common thread—providing diversions from the brutality and boredom of the war while reminding the soldiers of better times at home. Since the typical response from the men was enthusiastic, and many of them still remember fondly the work these women did, it is evident that the women succeeded in their efforts.

Chapter 4:
War Correspondents

The Vietnam War presented an opportunity for women journalists to escape narrow reporting roles that focused on so-called women's issues, such as fashion, high society news, cooking, and family. The Vietnam War was not the first covered by female war correspondents, but it was the first in which there were many women reporting. Among the thousands of credentialed journalists who were in South Vietnam at some point during the war, at least three dozen were women. They included combat photographers, essayists, high-profile interviewers, and broadcast journalists. Most of the women journalists in South Vietnam were American, but there were also Australians, as well as women from France and Germany.

"I Don't Do Weddings"

Female journalists had to overcome the traditional expectations of the men in charge of the media if they expected to get meaningful assignments in South Vietnam. Most men thought that combat was no place for a woman. Furthermore, most women in reporting had had little opportunity to pursue hard news stories, so they were thought to lack the experience and judgment to be good war reporters. Some men also assumed that women seeking war correspondent duties were frivolous, and would just be taking work from men. Essentially, the prevailing attitude among male journalists was that female war correspondents were not credible. Denby Fawcett, who worked for the *Honolulu Star-Bulletin* in 1966, encountered exactly these sorts of obstacles:

> I was [stuck] as a reporter on the . . . women's page, . . . [helping] cover Honolulu social events. My . . . editors thought I was joking when I asked them to free me from the society pages to cover the Vietnam War. They said it was out of the question, so I quit . . . and was ready to leave for Vietnam as a freelancer when, at the last minute, [the *Honolulu Advertiser* managing editor] took a chance and hired me as one of his reporters.[49]

"Find Me a Girl Reporter"

In her autobiography, *Fighting for Air: In the Trenches with Television News*, long-time television broadcast correspondent Liz Trotta gives the reader a vivid picture of what television journalism was like as the Vietnam War unfolded, and how difficult it was for women in broadcasting to get respect for their work. Trotta began working for NBC Television in April 1965. NBC's president had demanded his news division "find me a girl reporter" because a competing network had hired a woman. Trotta found she had to overcome male prejudice about a woman's ability to do the job. Even with management behind her, it was not easy. She had to find a way to gain the confidence of the cameramen and soundmen she would work with every day. In her autobiography, she wrote:

I wasn't a "girl reporter," but a reporter who happened to be a girl. [However,] I knew it wasn't going to be easy to convince the camera crews. . . . It was uphill all the way. Most were courteous, and . . . I learned [the nuances of the] camera from them. But unhappily, a [large] percentage of them couldn't handle a woman on the job. It wasn't until . . . I returned from my first war tour, that they . . . could comfortably accept [me].

Trotta spent about six months in South Vietnam as a television war correspondent, proving that a woman could excel at this competitive and dangerous job.

Reporter Liz Trotta of NBC encountered similar obstacles. In 1967, as television news expanded its coverage of the war, she lobbied for a position as a war correspondent for the network. Instead, one producer approached her about working on a network special report on the wedding of Lynda Bird Johnson, the daughter of President Lyndon Johnson. Trotta's assignment was to report on the wedding dress. She refused the assignment, saying, "But I don't do weddings. Don't you understand? I want to cover a war—not a wedding."[50] Time and again, it took the perseverance of the reporter to push against the obstacles put before her if she wanted to be a real war correspondent.

Sometimes men were reluctant to send women reporters to Vietnam out of concern for their safety. Tracy Wood, a reporter for United Press International, had this sort of trouble with her boss when she requested an assignment in

Vietnam. His feelings on placing her in the field were clear, as Wood later wrote:

He said, "I don't believe women should cover wars. . . . If anything happened to you, I'd feel bad." . . . [He] had just [stated] the problem that for generations held women back. Not overt sexual discrimination. Not conviction that women couldn't do the job. Something much harder to fight: well-meaning men in positions of authority who honestly believed it was more important to protect women from risks than encourage them to reach for the stars.[51]

Reporters in the Field

Women still confronted obstacles even after they got to Vietnam. Upon her arrival, Fawcett found she faced editorial restrictions common to many female reporters. She was promoted by the *Advertiser* as specializing in stories about style and living in Saigon, the capital of South Vietnam. She was supposed to restrict herself to features she could produce from the relative safety of Saigon, while a male reporter took care of coverage at the front. Only when that reporter went to another job was Fawcett able to become a full-fledged war correspondent.

Once in the field, women reporters found that military officers often treated them with disrespect. Some officers would insist on precautions that made the reporter's job more difficult. The Marine Corps, for example, often required escorts for women reporters, though there was no such requirement for male correspondents. Reporter Jurate Kazickas, who worked for a number of small publications, was extremely fit and an experienced backpacker, but the U.S. Marine Corps required her to be accompanied by a male sergeant when she went on a long-range recon patrol with a company of marines. Kazickas kept up with the troops on the grueling march. Ironically, her escort, who was out of shape, injured himself. Consequently, the commanding officer ordered them both evacuated by helicopter halfway through the patrol.

A woman reporter might also encounter a problem by triggering a personal reaction from the officer. Denby Fawcett was once refused access to the front line because the commanding officer said she reminded him of his daughter. Other times, the men in charge were dishonest about their concerns; Fawcett was not allowed on a helicopter in one instance on the pretense that it had too much weight on board already, even though she weighed only 110 pounds and the helicopter was lightly loaded. Commanders often expressed concern that a woman's presence at the front would be a distraction to the troops. Kazickas, faced with such an objection, said, "Your men are professionals. They'll

Sexist attitudes caused many officers to treat female war correspondents like Denby Fawcett with overt disrespect.

do the right thing. Besides, I can take care of myself."[52] On the other hand, the occasional officer would actually try to turn the woman into a distraction, hoping to improve his soldiers' morale. This lack of respect was intolerable for most women correspondents, who were just trying to do their jobs.

The most serious threat to women reporters' ability to report on the war came out of a chance encounter in 1967 between Denby Fawcett and General William Westmoreland, then the commander of American ground forces in Vietnam. Fawcett had spent several days and nights at a remote base in South Vietnam's Central Highlands to report on Hawaiian troops. Westmoreland conducted an inspection while she was there and recognized her, because he had known her parents. Apparently alarmed at the notion of a young woman he knew being put at risk with combat troops, he considered ordering that women reporters could not stay overnight at bases on the front lines. Because of the difficulty of getting into and out of these bases, this order would have effectively excluded women from almost all combat reporting roles. Two other female correspondents, Anne Morrissy and Ann Bryan, lobbied the Defense Department to stop the rule from being implemented. They were supported by all the other American

Marguerite Higgins

❦

When young female journalists in America first began to think about going to Vietnam to report on the war, some of them were certainly inspired by Marguerite Higgins. She was the most prominent female war correspondent of the 1950s, famous for her coverage of combat in Korea. She also spent significant time in Vietnam covering the French conflict with the Viet Minh.

Higgins later made several trips to South Vietnam as a reporter. She had to be evacuated back to the United States in 1965, ill with the tropical disease that would soon kill her. She had reported not only on the combat, but also on the politics. Her book *Our Vietnam Nightmare*

Marguerite Higgins was the most prominent female correspondent during the Korean War.

predicted the failure of American involvement in South Vietnam. This book proved Higgins to be more than a reporter. Her ability to explain and analyze the details of the conflict was invaluable to anyone seeking an understanding of the complexities of Vietnam. It was a great loss for journalism when she died at the age of forty-seven.

women reporters in Vietnam and succeeded in keeping the opportunity to get close to combat troops.

Print Journalists

Once they overcame gender-related prejudices, women demonstrated they could be effective war correspondents. They worked for major wire services such as United Press International (UPI) and Associated Press (AP); major newspapers, including the *New York Times*, *New York Herald Tribune*, *Christian Science Monitor*, and *Washington Post*; smaller newspapers; national magazines like *Time* and *Newsweek*; news syndicates; and small-circulation magazines. Some were employed directly by publications or services, others were stringers (journalists working with a particular publication or service, but only paid for articles accepted), and some operated as true freelancers, selling their work wherever they could.

Women became war correspondents in Vietnam in a variety of ways. A few were veteran war correspondents. Reporter Martha Gellhorn, for example, had been reporting on wars since the 1930s, while reporter Marguerite Higgins reported from the front lines during World War II and the Korean War. Higgins was also the first American woman to report from Vietnam, as she covered the French military in North Vietnam in 1953. Altogether, she went to Vietnam ten times.

Other women had no experience at all but managed to succeed anyway. Reporter Kate Webb, for example, had a difficult time getting started in Vietnam. She had been working in Australia for a newspaper in a nonreporting job, and at the age of twenty-three decided to go to Vietnam to be a war correspondent. She did this without first lining up any work, or finding out how reporters worked there, or even what the cost of living was. She arrived in Saigon in March 1967. "I quickly realized that my few dollars wouldn't last in a place where 'war correspondents' . . . [spent] at least as much time in expensive cocktail lounges as in foxholes, and after the first few weeks, I was hanging on by my teeth."[53]

Webb first wrote articles for Vietnamese English-language newspapers for a few cents an article, which barely gave her enough money to buy noodle soup from street vendors. A little later she was able to string for an alternative American soldiers' newspaper, the *Overseas Weekly*, which also got her accreditation with the Military Assistance Command in Vietnam. This accreditation meant she was officially a journalist in the eyes of the U.S. military. Her progress was still difficult. For a while she spent most of her time in Saigon, doing hometowners (articles sold to the newspapers in the soldiers' hometowns in America about individual soldiers) as a UPI stringer. After more than a year, she finally established herself as one of UPI's most accomplished reporters, with articles published in the *New York Times* and *Newsweek*.

Photojournalists

Although most women war correspondents concentrated on creating written accounts of the war, almost every woman reporter also took photographs as the opportunity arose. Photos could give more meaning to an article, and a good photo could be sold even if there was no more than a caption to go with it.

Perhaps half a dozen women combat journalists relied primarily on their cameras and picture-taking skills. Some were veterans who had begun in the 1940s and 1950s, while others took up the profession only after getting to Vietnam. This might have been the most difficult journalism job in Vietnam, because the most dramatic photo opportunities often occurred at the most dangerous moments in combat. Women whose natural inclination might have been to seek cover instead sought to cover the war with their cameras. Liz Trotta of NBC described this internal conflict as she covered a fight in Tay Ninh Province. She wrote,

[My cameraman said,] "You either get it—or you don't." . . . I froze in place. The idea was for me to make up my mind right there whether or not I was going to be a combat correspondent. To this day I don't know if he meant get the picture or get killed, but in either case it holds: you simply have to move out and take your chances, when all common sense is telling you to run and hide.[54]

One of the two veteran female photojournalists in Vietnam was Frenchwoman Cathy Leroy, one of the best combat photographers of the war. She was in combat in South Vietnam almost constantly throughout the sixties. Gloria Emerson, a *New York Times* correspondent in South Vietnam, wrote, "[Leroy] became a legend . . . for her astonishing courage, tough tongue, and persist-

ence. The troops loved her."[55] The other veteran woman photographer, Dicky Chappelle, continued in South Vietnam a career she began in World War II as perhaps the first female combat photojournalist.

A few other women, such as German-born Rena Briand, took up photojournalism for the first time in Vietnam. Starting in 1965 with nothing more than a good camera and encouragement from friends, she was soon selling her photographs to AP and continued to do so until she left in 1967.

Several women television reporters served in South Vietnam, and others worked in radio—both of these are referred to as broadcast journalism. Broadcast journalism was still fairly new when the Vietnam War began. The standards for television journalism in particular were still evolving as the war became more intense, and the opportunities for reporting were limited.

Female television reporters encountered many of the same problems that women print journalists did, but television news made the task of reporting more complicated. For one thing, the job was dependent on equipment; if the movie camera or sound equipment failed, it could ruin the story. The reporter also had to coordinate with the cameraman and the soundman, in contrast to print journalists who worked on

North Vietnamese Reporters

In contrast to the relatively well-known Western female journalists who came to Vietnam, little is known about specific North Vietnamese and Viet Cong women reporters during the war. A few women served as war correspondents for the Vietnam News Agency (VNA) or its Viet Cong–based counterpart, the Liberation News Agency (LNA). Lacking the equipment and transportation alternatives of Western reporters in South Vietnam, VNA and LNA reporters had to send back their stories and photographs to the north by the Ho Chi Minh Trail, a network of trails that provided the main supply connection between North and South Vietnam. Because most of the traffic on the trail was by foot, this meant it took at least three months for the material to be published in North Vietnam, and sometimes longer.

The VNA and LNA women were known to assist in the secret publication of pamphlets and newsletters for distribution in South Vietnam. They and their male compatriots maintained printing and photo-developing equipment in the field. Two women photographers who worked in these hidden facilities were Le Thi Nang, who was killed in an air attack while working as a darkroom technician in 1972, and Ngoc Huong, killed during the Tet Offensive in 1968.

their own. It was probably the most complex task for a field journalist anywhere.

"I Guess It Was Bound to Happen"

Like all occupations in Vietnam, reporting from the front was a dangerous business for women. More than any other noncombatants, women war correspondents were faced with the same battlefield risks that combat soldiers endured. Inevitably, women journalists were injured, and killed, in combat. At least one became a prisoner. Apart from combat injuries, all ran the risk of catching dangerous tropical diseases, and they were often exposed to toxic chemicals.

More women reporters suffered from serious diseases than combat wounds. Apart from tropical diseases like malaria, there were also increased risks of infection in Vietnam and the risk of exposure to poisonous defoliants (plant-killing chemicals) like Agent Orange. For example, reporter Marguerite Higgins contracted leishmaniasis, a parasitic tropical disease and, although evacuated to the United States for treatment, died in early 1966 at the age of forty-seven. Other women war correspondents also suffered from diseases. Denby Fawcett wrote,

> I left Vietnam in 1967, exhausted and sick. . . . I didn't know I was sick then; I thought the war had made me crazy. Anything slightly sad would make me cry. . . . My

weariness I attributed to personal depression over the hopelessness of Vietnam. I would slap my face to [stay] awake as I struggled to write stories, working a little and then slumping over my typewriter.[56]

When she returned to Hawaii, her illness was eventually diagnosed as a dangerous form of malaria. It took her two months of treatment to recover.

Reporter Tad Bartimus, working for AP, developed a mysterious condition in

Many war correspondents contracted serious tropical diseases. Denby Fawcett left Vietnam with a virulent form of malaria and needed months to recover.

War Correspondents

1974 which left her exhausted, coughing, and complaining of joint pains. Her condition was eventually diagnosed as an autoimmune disease (where the person's own immune system reacts against the body), probably caused by her exposure to Agent Orange while she was in Vietnam. This same defoliant has also been implicated in illnesses of many other Vietnam veterans and in birth defects of their children.

Combat injuries to women correspondents were rare but did occur. Photographer Dicky Chappelle was the only American woman war correspondent to be killed in combat. In 1965 she was on a patrol with U.S. Marines when a land mine exploded nearby. She bled to death in a matter of minutes. Her last words were reportedly "I guess it was bound to happen."[57] Jurate Kazickas was almost crippled for life. On March 7, 1968, she was at Khe Sanh, the site of some of the most vicious fighting of the war. An artillery shell exploded near her; shrapnel hit her in the face, legs, and buttocks. The last injury was just a fraction of an inch from her spine. She wrote, "I was unbelievably lucky, for had it been any closer, I might have been seriously disabled. [Instead], I was merely mortified."[58]

Perhaps the most harrowing experience any woman journalist had in Vietnam was that of United Press International correspondent Kate Webb, who was captured by the North Vietnamese in April 1971. She and several other reporters were held prisoner for twenty-three days, by which time her agency

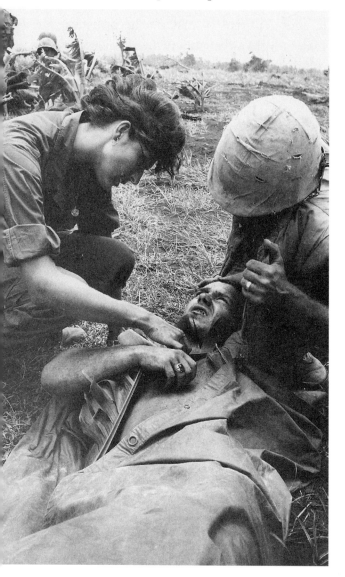

War correspondent Jurate Kazickas (pictured comforting a wounded soldier) was nearly crippled when an artillery shell exploded near her.

assumed she was dead. In fact, a body was misidentified as hers, and her parents had already held a memorial service before she regained her freedom. Webb was in very bad shape by the time she and her companions were released. She suffered from malnutrition, severely infected feet, and two strains of malaria, but was able to fully recover.

Objectivity and Involvement

Reporters are taught to report on stories, not become part of them. In the intense conditions of the Vietnam War, this was often easier said than done. Indeed, maintaining objectivity is extremely difficult in normal reporting situations, and even more so when reporting on something as controversial and engaging as a war.

For most war correspondents, personal involvement with the people they reported on was inevitable. In some cases, women reporters had no choice but to get involved with their subjects. Kazickas recalls,

Very often, I would put down my camera and help with the wounded, for which I was severely criticized by some of my colleagues. "We heard you played Florence Nightingale [a famous combat nurse from the nineteenth century] on that patrol." But there was a point where I could not continue to [be emotionally detached]. . . . You just threw down your camera and wrapped bandages.[59]

In some other cases, friendship inspired women correspondents to do things outside the reporter's role. Liz Trotta recalled her departure from one fire base where she had befriended the soldiers she was supposed to be reporting on. "Good-bye time, addresses and phone numbers exchanged, another soldier became brother and buddy for a few hours."[60] Another reporter, Laura Palmer, was fired by her employer, ABC, because her friendships had become public and appeared to indicate bias. During a cease-fire in 1973, for example, Palmer was photographed shaking hands with two Viet Cong women, and the pictures were sent all over the world by UPI.

Objectivity was always difficult in this very difficult war. Women reporters witnessed brutality and destruction, injury and death, on a regular basis, and most of them came to see it as a great waste. Even if they were opposed to the war, however, most of the women reporters were committed as professionals to reporting objectively.

Chapter 5:
Women Combatants

More women may have fought in the Vietnam War than any other war in history. Almost all of the combatant women were Vietnamese. By contrast, none of the women from the Western nations were trained or deployed as combat soldiers. Most of the Western women in the military were nurses; a handful had other occupations relating to the command and control of American forces. Some Western women had been trained in the use of firearms; a few took up arms under extraordinary circumstances. Vietnamese women, however, made significant military contributions to their side's war effort.

The North Vietnamese Army

When the United States and its allies entered the war, North Vietnam was forced to bring large numbers of women into the armed forces. The north simply did not have the manpower to continue its offensive against South Vietnam and at the same time defend North Vietnam itself. Although women had been directly involved in military actions since the struggle against the French after World War II, they rarely took part in actual combat. As the war went on, however, it became evident to the Communist regime that there would not be enough men to fight. They thus asked women to volunteer in 1965 and again in 1966.

The response from women was greater than expected. A single village district in North Vietnam might have had a quota of two hundred volunteers, but as many as two thousand came forward. There are no reliable reports of the total number of women volunteers, but it was at least a quarter of a million for the period between 1965 and 1972. Many of these women were trained for combat and were placed into all-female units. The women then went to the south to fight just as their male counterparts did.

The women faced some prejudice from men in the army. One commanding officer, a man, wrote, "I decided to keep only the fittest [soldiers] and to transfer the girls back to the second line.

Girls could be good at bookkeeping, handling freight, or even managing antiaircraft guns. But they would be no match for Saigon infantry."[61] However, his opinion was not universal among male commanders. Other commanders felt that women made fine soldiers, and that revolutionary will was more important than physical strength.

Transportation and Supply

By far the largest number of women soldiers were those who helped to maintain the Ho Chi Minh Trail and to move supplies along it. There might have been as many as 180,000 noncombatant women serving in transportation and supply jobs during the course of the war. Although these women were not trained for combat, they faced as many risks as true combat-trained soldiers, and in some cases their situation was more dangerous.

The primary work of these women was to maintain and expand the Ho Chi Minh Trail, a network of tracks that led from North Vietnam to South Vietnam, through difficult jungle and mountain terrain. The trail was essential to supplying Communist insurgents in South

A North Vietnamese woman teaches a group of teenage girls to fire a rifle. Large numbers of North Vietnamese women volunteered for all-female combat units.

Women Combatants

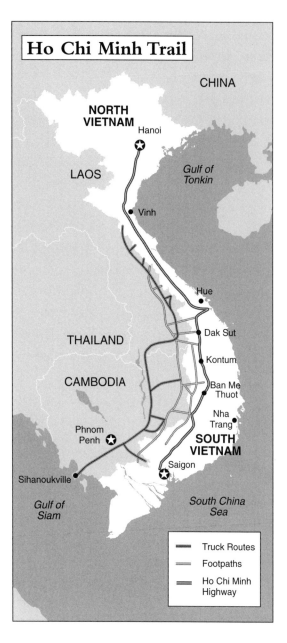

Ho Chi Minh Trail

CHINA

NORTH VIETNAM

Hanoi

LAOS

Gulf of Tonkin

Vinh

Hue

THAILAND

Dak Sut

Kontum

CAMBODIA

Ban Me Thuot

Nha Trang

Phnom Penh

SOUTH VIETNAM

Saigon

Sihanoukville

Gulf of Siam

South China Sea

— Truck Routes
═ Footpaths
━ Ho Chi Minh Highway

stretches of road. The U.S. military caused further damage by constantly bombing the trail. They left craters everywhere, some of which had delayed-action or dud bombs in them. Fixing the trail in the wake of this destruction was the job of the youth brigades, who were between 40 and 70 percent women. Usually the youths had nothing to work with except shovels, hoes, and other hand tools.

Maintenance of the existing trails took up most of the effort of the brigades. Where flooding or mudslides damaged a trail, the labor was difficult but straight-forward. When bombs were involved, no work could begin until sappers cleared unexploded bombs. Sappers were people who were specially trained to detonate, defuse, or remove unexploded bombs. This dangerous job often fell to women, perhaps because it required precision rather than strength. In some cases they would use dynamite to blow up unexploded bombs. One of the first women to do this was Nguyen Thi Lieu, part of an all-female platoon of sappers. She reportedly deactivated more bombs than the rest of her team. One soldier commented to someone who did not know Lieu, "Haven't you ever heard of Lieu, head of the volunteer platoon at Ta Le? Six times she and her friends were buried under bomb-triggered landslides and each time they

Vietnam. Some of the tracks could take trucks, others only bicycles, and some were strictly footpaths. Nothing was paved. During the rainy season, roads would wash out, bridges would collapse in floods, and avalanches would block managed to get out and go on with their work."[62] Lieu's luck finally ran out; one of the bombs killed her.

Sappers were not the only ones at risk. The women maintaining the trail were also attacked by bombs. American aircraft dropped various small antipersonnel bombs and mines as well as the larger bombs designed to wreck roads and bridges. Sometimes these small bombs were concealed and only went off when touched or stepped on. Many women of the youth brigades lost feet or hands to these tiny weapons as they attempted to repair the road, while others were killed outright. The Americans also dropped napalm and sprayed defoliants like Agent Orange. These burned or poisoned the vegetation, eliminating the cover of the jungle and limiting the ability of the North Vietnamese to forage for food.

The damage to the roads was the biggest obstacle caused by American bombing. Huge bomb craters made it difficult for trucks to travel roads and deliver much-needed supplies. Roads were exceptionally difficult to navigate at night, which was when most trucks usually moved to avoid detection. Women helped direct traffic through damaged sections of the road, helping

The Tet Offensive

The Vietnamese lunar new year's festival, Tet, is a time of celebration in Vietnam. The Viet Cong and North Vietnamese chose to take advantage of relaxed vigilance during the holiday on January 31, 1968, to stage a massive offensive all across South Vietnam. Seventy thousand Communists attacked dozens of cities, towns, and military bases.

The offensive was devastating for both sides. More than fifty thousand Communists died, among them many women. Many civilians were killed, especially in Hue, where the Communists massacred thousands of men, women, and children. The ARVN and U.S. forces also suffered combined deaths in excess of six thousand. Property damage was also massive; Hue in particular was almost leveled.

In purely military terms, Tet was a defeat for the North Vietnamese and the Viet Cong. However, it turned out to be an unexpected political triumph for the Communists, as it provided horrific images for television, and marked the point at which American public opinion began to turn away permanently from supporting the war.

the trucks avoid the bomb craters and other obstacles in their path. The women would wear white so that the truck drivers could see them better in the dim conditions.

Women also operated as couriers to move supplies along the trail. In most cases, women, some as young as thirteen, worked side by side with men. They might balance loads of several hundred pounds on bicycles that they walked along the trails, or they might have carried loads of fifty pounds or more on their backs.

Supplies were very tight, and what there was had to be conserved to move forward to the soldiers fighting in South Vietnam. Most of the women had an inadequate diet, especially for the strenuous work they were doing. Some accidentally poisoned themselves by eating mushrooms or fruits that were toxic. Others tried to survive on what little rice they could get, supplemented by leaves or grass. Even when they had rice, they had to be careful about cooking it, · as the American aircraft could detect the heat of cooking fires with infrared sensors and bomb them. Often the North Vietnamese road crews could not cook for weeks at a time.

Because they got so little nourishment, the youth brigade women were especially susceptible to disease. Malaria was the biggest problem. It probably caused or contributed to more deaths among the North Vietnamese women roadworkers than all other causes combined. It is estimated that 20 percent of those on the Ho Chi Minh Trail were killed, but only 2 percent of those deaths were from bombs. Women got sick more often than men, but seemed to be less likely to die from disease. At any given time, between 20 and 80 percent of a road crew would be ill with malaria or some other serious malady. Even so, many women worked until they literally dropped from weakness. Many women who did not die suffered long-term health problems, such as infertility or chronic malaria. If they seemed sickly, they could not find men willing to marry them, and with infertility problems, they either could not have children, or the children were born with birth defects. In these circumstances, the women affected were burdened long after the war, some for the rest of their lives.

Home Defense Units

Even as a million or more women went into combat or helped maintain the supply of the combat troops, someone had to defend North Vietnam itself. There were some regular army units with men in the north, and men also exclusively staffed Vietnam's very small navy and air force. Men were also the only ones to

Women in a North Vietnamese militia unit operate an antiaircraft gun. Female artillery units in North Vietnam were responsible for shooting down several U.S. aircraft.

maintain and fire the guided missile defenses of North Vietnam. Almost every other branch of home and civil defense, however, was made up largely of women.

Substantial numbers of women were armed as part of the militia, along with overage men and those not fit for army service. These units would have provided backup to regular army units if there had been an invasion of North Vietnam. As this never happened, militia members focused on the capture of American crewmen from aircraft shot down over North Vietnam. They also found and guarded aircraft wreckage until it could be dealt with by regular army troops. Apart from these duties, they assisted in repairs and rescue operations after air raids.

Most of the antiaircraft guns were staffed partially or entirely by militia-women. These weapons required from two to twenty crew members, depending on their size and complexity. Most were either heavy machine guns or rapid-fire small-caliber cannons. When fired these guns used up ammunition very rapidly. One of the most important jobs, therefore, was to keep supplying gunners with ammunition. One woman, militiawoman Ngo Thi Tuyen, won fame for carrying two boxes of ammunition that together weighed 98 kilograms, or about 216 pounds. This was twice her own weight. During that two-day period in 1965 she also aided wounded comrades, moved other supplies, prepared food for the gun crews, and helped dig trenches to shelter the gun crews and others from the constant bombing. For this and for later efforts, she was eventually declared a Hero of the People's Armed Forces.

Women fired the guns too. For example, one sixteen-woman platoon near Hanoi, all between the ages of seventeen and twenty, was credited with shooting down several aircraft. They did better with their heavy cannons than did the old men who manned nearby guns. The men could not see as well, and were not agile enough to aim the guns quickly.

In fact, at times it seemed that practically every man and woman in Hanoi was armed against the airborne intruders. *New York Times* reporter Harrison Salisbury was in Hanoi during the winter of 1966–1967; he observed that "every other person was carrying a gun . . . strapped to his or her back. When the air alert sounded, rifles appeared in every hand. Petite . . . waitresses at the hotel suddenly donned tin helmets, grabbed their rifles and rushed to the rooftops."[63]

Women and Civil Defense

Women took a major role in civil defense. Civil defense is organized work by civilians to protect people and property from attacks, and to repair damage from such attacks. They helped build bomb shelters, including digging one-person manhole-covered wells that flanked the streets of Hanoi. They organized to rescue people trapped by debris after air raids, which was especially important because the victims could quickly suffocate or be crushed by further collapse of a damaged building. Women cleared debris from roads, sometimes using nothing more than their bare hands. Historian Albert Marrin writes, "Each person, depending upon age and ability, was given a specific task to make him or her feel part of the war effort. In addition to your regular job, you might serve with a fire brigade, join a first-aid team or ambulance unit, repair bomb damage or defuse unexploded bombs."[64]

Women were especially important in rendering first aid and in collecting the dead. In the case of emergency medical aid, they had only the most rudimentary supplies and training, but they were organized ahead of time and quickly mobilized after an air raid. Phan Thanh Hao, then a teenager in Hanoi and later a journalist, recalls her own experience: "We girls . . . had to learn military training and nurses' training, [and first aid techniques]. . . . We learned only simple methods."[65] Hao and others learned to cope with recovering bodies, which was important both to preserve the public health and to give the families of the deceased an opportunity to conduct proper funeral services, considered very important in Vietnamese culture.

All in all, North Vietnamese women made all sorts of contributions during the war. This widespread participation by North Vietnamese women was critical to the perseverance of North Vietnam throughout the war.

A North Vietnamese woman sounds an air-raid alarm. Throughout the war, Vietnamese women played a major role in all areas of civil defense.

The Long-Haired Army

The Communists in South Vietnam also depended on women to a large degree. The Viet Cong were not originally part of the North Vietnamese Army; they

South Vietnamese police question a suspected Viet Cong sympathizer at gunpoint. The Viet Cong was comprised largely of women drawn from every sector of society.

were almost entirely men and women from the south, and were the military arm of the National Liberation Front (NLF), which had first combined Communist and non-Communist opposition groups. After 1967 North Vietnamese, including many women, became part of the Viet Cong to make up for losses among the southerners, and the NLF became more directly subservient to North Vietnam. Although it is impossible to document exact numbers, most sources estimate that there were more women than men in the Viet Cong. In fact, women may have comprised 70

percent of the total. These estimates can be very broad, including everyone from casual informants to political cadres (a small unit of Communists skilled in political teaching) to combat troops, all roles filled by women. Perhaps 1 to 2 million women were involved with the Viet Cong in some capacity. They were collectively known in Vietnam as "the long-haired army."

Some Vietnamese women gathered information about ARVN and U.S. troop movements, operations, and capabilities. The women were from every part of Vietnamese society; mama-sans, brothel owners, high school students, wives of doctors or prosperous merchants, and peasants with sharp eyes were all among the information collectors. Many of these women were only peripherally involved with the Viet Cong; they supplied information on an irregular basis, spending most of their time living their usual lifestyle. Their reasons for helping varied. They might have secretly sympathized with the goals of the NLF. They might have helped because a loved one was being held hostage by the Viet Cong. They might not care particularly for the Communists, but were strongly opposed to the South Vietnamese government. Some simply traded their services for cash. Other women were full-time Viet Cong. These latter made an effort to spy on enemy forces, often looking for specific information.

Women also often served as couriers. The Viet Cong had few radios and no telephones, so information had to be delivered by hand. Women could move about more freely than men, as they were less likely to be suspected of being Viet Cong, especially by American troops, and thus less likely to be stopped and searched. Women also often moved supplies for the Viet Cong, as there was little to distinguish a woman carrying food to market from one carrying food to the Viet Cong.

Women were also important members of political cadres. These groups educated peasants about the corruption and unfairness of the South Vietnamese regime and about the benefits of becoming part of the Communist uprising. Political cadres helped the Viet Cong get new recruits constantly and earned the support of the peasants in the countryside. Women were often a prominent part of a cadre.

The cadres followed a specific process in attempting to convert villagers to support the Viet Cong. Women often spoke to other women, offering perspective that a man might not be able to offer. A cadre might visit a village several times. On the first visit, they would offer help; women cadre members often provided minor medical aid, for example. They put on entertainment that criticized the government; one common practice was to put monkeys in costumes, liken them to leaders of the South Vietnamese government and then release the monkeys in the middle of the village. A woman cadre member might offer a running commentary on the government leaders in a mocking tone, while the monkeys scampered all over the village, screaming and getting into everything. Finally, cadre members would suggest how the peasants' lot could improve, asking leading questions that always alluded to government incompetence and corruption. In subsequent visits, the same cadre would reemphasize the previous messages. In this way, people were recruited to join the Viet Cong.

Ut Tich

A mong the Viet Cong and the North Vietnamese, Ut Tich was a legend. She was known as "the fighting mother," for being a frontline guerrilla, while giving birth to six children over the course of the war. Despite having many children, she was reputed to be a full-time guerrilla, away from home from dawn to late at night. It is said that she began her pro-Communist belligerence at age fourteen by attacking an abusive landlord with a knife. She remained single for some time but eventually fell in love with a soldier, who taught her how to throw grenades. She is credited with killing dozens of the enemy from ambush and was notorious for her capacity for revenge.

The only primary sources describing Ut Tich's career are official publications from North Vietnam, whose officials could have fabricated details or the whole story for propaganda purposes. If the stories are true, Ut Tich was certainly one of the fiercest and most dedicated warriors of either gender in the war.

Cadres were also often responsible for collecting the funds that the Viet Cong needed to operate. Women were considered more persuasive in this role and also more likely to be ignored by enemy soldiers or police. Minimizing the risk of search was important since someone dressed as a peasant but possessing a large quantity of cash would be suspicious. With enough money the Viet Cong could buy goods on the black market.

Fighting for the Viet Cong

Sabotage and assassination were also activities undertaken by women Viet Cong. Viet Cong women undertook drive-by bombings of bars and restaurants in Saigon by throwing grenades through open doors from the backs of motor scooters. They also committed drive-by murders of American troops on leave in Saigon. Some posed as street vendors and injured soldiers by selling soft drinks contaminated with ground glass, or beer mixed with battery acid. Women were primarily responsible for the manufacture and planting of deadly booby traps in places where soldiers were likely to go. They were also sometimes a part of teams that would go to the homes of those who had defected from the Viet Cong, to execute the defector. They took part in political assassinations as well, killing corrupt village chiefs, schoolteachers, and social workers—essentially, any and all government officials and employees. Apparently, some of the women on these assassination squads were more ruthless than the men.

Women Viet Cong certainly served in combat. It is impossible to say what proportion of the fighting forces they comprised. Even most of those who mainly cooked or carried supplies or collected taxes had rifles. Photos of dead Viet Cong fighters usually show only men, although there are many pictures of armed or captured Viet Cong women. Some, such as Ut Tich, had reputations as fierce killers.

Women commanded in the Viet Cong and the NLF, though they were certainly in the minority in this capacity. Ut Tich, for example, was renowned as a combat commander. Other women were fairly high in the command structure. One of the highest ranked leaders of the Viet Cong was Nguyen Thi Dinh. She was deputy commander in chief of the Viet Cong at one point, which placed her second in the line of command. Another woman, Duong Quynh Hoa, held the title of deputy minister of health in the Provisional Revolutionary Government, the NLF's shadowy alternative to the government in power in Saigon. These women's accomplishments stand as a reflection of how important women were to the overall successes of the Viet Cong and are especially remarkable in light of the prevailing attitude in the south that women ought to be subservient to men.

South Vietnamese Women in the Military

Compared with the Communists, the South Vietnamese regime used few women in combat. Nevertheless, some women did take up arms in defense of South Vietnam. Other women were involved militarily without being fighting troops themselves.

Madame Ngo Dinh Nhu sponsored one of the earliest female military units, the Paramilitary Women of Vietnam. Madame Nhu used the Trung sisters (two women from Vietnam's ancient past who led an army of insurrection against the invading Chinese) as an inspiration to her recruits. At the time, there was no particular need for more South Vietnamese military units, but Madame Nhu was trying to advance the social position of women by demonstrating their competence. She felt that "if women have their own army, they have a better chance to obtain their own rights."[66] The paramilitary women were taught how to use firearms and in one contest were reputed to have shot more accurately than men from an ARVN unit. They formed village defense forces, but when the November 1963 coup d'état (an internal insurrection) overthrew

Madame Nhu—the Dragon Lady

Madame Ngo Dinh Nhu was the only woman to achieve significant political power in South Vietnam. She was the sister-in-law of South Vietnam's first president, Ngo Dinh Diem, married to his closest adviser, his brother Nhu. Because Diem never married, Madame Nhu became the unofficial first lady of the regime.

Madame Nhu was nicknamed "the Dragon Lady," due to her strongly held conservative beliefs and fiery public statements. She had no official government position, but her influence over Diem was very strong. He shared her conservative attitudes. Even when she overstepped the bounds of his policies, he refused to rebuke her, because he would not publicly show tension within his family. At her insistence, abortion, divorce, polygamy, concubinage, contraception, and dancing were all prohibited, and bar girls were made to wear conservative clothing. These bans were at odds with the permissive side of Vietnamese culture, and so she was disliked by many.

Madame Nhu was tactless in her public statements and did not understand the furor she caused. Her most infamous speech came after the protest suicide by fire of a Buddhist monk. According to Stanley Karnow in *Vietnam: A History*, she said the Buddhists had done nothing but "barbecue a monk. . . . Let them burn, and we shall clap our hands." This appalled both Americans and Vietnamese.

In the fall of 1963 Madame Nhu began a speaking tour through the United States, making controversial statements at every stop. Her own father trailed her throughout America, contradicting her and criticizing Diem's regime as worse than the Communists'. In the midst of this controversy, President Diem and Madame Nhu's husband were overthrown by the ARVN and murdered. Madame Nhu went into exile in Europe; she spent the rest of her life there.

Madame Ngo Dinh Nhu was an important political figure in South Vietnam in the early years of the war.

President Diem and Madame Nhu's husband, these units were disbanded by the new regime.

The Paramilitary Women of Vietnam was eventually reinstated by a future regime, however. Over time, it evolved into the ARVN Women's Armed Forces Corps (WAFC), fashioned after a similar arrangement in the U.S. Army. It is unclear to what extent the WAFCs saw combat, though it is evident that some did.

On the other hand, many South Vietnamese women served in a combat role in the militia (local defense forces), particularly after 1967. There was more than one militia organization, but they were all similar in that they were composed primarily of peasants who, when necessary, defended the area in which they lived but otherwise continued to work. This arrangement worked fairly well for women, who did not have to be separated from their family while in military service. The men and women in the militias were neither well trained nor given much in the way of military equipment, but because they were defending their homes and families, they were sometimes more effective against the Communists than was the ARVN.

Western Women and Military Activity

None of the Western military or civilian women in Vietnam were given extensive combat training as were Vietnamese women. On occasion, women informally learned how to use military weapons, and in a few instances used them in combat. A handful of women in the military were involved in the actual conduct of the war, but they were not on the front lines.

Civilian women sometimes carried personal weapons. A few already knew how to handle guns before they came to Vietnam. Some women journalists carried pistols, though most did not. They tended to believe that having a gun would do them little good, and in any event, they were there to get a story, not shoot people.

One woman journalist, Australian Jan Graham, did fire a weapon in combat. As she was traveling with two American soldiers, their jeep was ambushed. They took cover, and one soldier handed her a rifle. Other forces came to their aid, but Graham had fired the gun once or twice. The soldiers with her insisted that she killed one of the Viet Cong and showed her the body, but she was not convinced that she really shot him.

Another Australian woman, entertainer and performer Ingrid Hart, practiced with the standard rifle, the M-16, and became fairly good at hitting tin cans. When one of her acts was supposed to drive through potentially Viet Cong–occupied territory to reach a remote American base, nobody was assigned as the rear gunner for the last vehicle of the convoy. Hart took an M-16 and filled in. She said, "I'm 100 percent sure I would have shot [it if necessary].... I realise now the feeling of survival, what you don't ever realise in civilian life—it was either them or me."[67]

Some women were indirectly involved in combat. For example, journalist Denby Fawcett called in an air strike by radio for marines she was with, so that the marines could impress the navy pilots that they had an American woman in their camp. Reporter Kate Webb also called in one air strike, but it was under much more serious conditions. When the fighting in Vietnam spilled into Cambodia, the AP journalist went there; she was with a Cambodian army unit that became surrounded by North Vietnamese. The Americans flying air cover could not understand the French of the Cambodian commander well enough to bomb the enemy, so the Cambodian had Webb call in the air strike in English.

"A Little Less Helpless"

Army nurses were given limited training in the use of the .45-caliber pistol, but most never practiced with it. Very few nurses were even issued sidearms when in Vietnam. Army nurse Sara McVicker

insisted on getting some training when her orders came through to go to Vietnam and became a very good shot with a rifle. She said, "You know, I think it made me feel a little less helpless about being able to protect myself if worse came to worse."[68]

Nurses were not the only American women to serve in the military in Vietnam. Women's Army Corps members (WACs), Navy women (officially designated Women Accepted for Voluntary Emergency Service, or WAVES) and women marines (WMs) filled a variety of office and technical roles from the most secure locations in South Vietnam. Some three dozen WMs and about the same number of WAVES served in Vietnam at one point or another. About seven hundred WACs served in Vietnam in roles relating to communications, training, secretarial work, supply, data processing, protocol, personnel, and intelligence analysis. These women were generally the most protected of the women in the military in Vietnam, as they worked in very secure military facilities and were housed in areas protected even from their male compatriots. At least one WAC was injured by hostile fire, and others, while off base, saw men wounded or killed, but for the most part WACs were as isolated from combat as anyone could be in Vietnam.

Doris Allen

Doris I. "Lucki" Allen was one of the few African American women in the army to have military responsibilities during the time of the Vietnam War. She faced prejudice along the way, but fought through it to make a real contribution to the war effort.

Allen went to Vietnam in 1967 as an intelligence analyst (*intelligence* in a military context is the collection and analysis of information). This was desk work; she did not act as a spy. She remained there until 1970, far longer than the typical one-year tour. She volunteered because she felt she could contribute, as revealed in Keith Walker's book, *A Piece of My Heart: The Stories of Twenty-Six American Women Who Died in Vietnam:* "Knowing that I had an expertise that was needed, it was better for me to be there. Not to fight and not to shoot guns and not to kill people, but I looked at it rather that my intelligence would save lives." That is exactly what happened.

Allen analyzed information which revealed the impending Tet Offensive. Her warning was ignored because of her low rank, her race, and her gender, but Allen's accurate prediction established her reputation. She particularly warned about Viet Cong use of poison gas shells. This warning saved many lives when an officer found an undetonated chemical shell and kept his troops away. She also identified the probable location of a cache of rockets aimed at her own base, which the army then destroyed before they could be launched.

Allen was pleased to contribute to the war effort, but also felt frustrated with the effort she had to make to be heard. As an African American, a woman, and an enlisted person dealing with white male officers, she had to be persistent and forceful to overcome her superiors' unjustified preconceptions. It is fortunate for many that she was.

All in all, women proved to be very adaptable when asked to assume military roles. While many of these women did not actually have to go into combat, they all took on increased responsibility beyond their civilian roles, and for the most part they were effective contributors to their nation's war effort.

Chapter 6:
Protesting the War

❦

The war in Vietnam resonated deeply and negatively with many women, leading them to oppose the war. Women were a major factor in the protest movements in South Vietnam, America, and Australia. These movements were also a prelude to social and political change relating to women's rights in America and Australia.

Protests by Vietnamese

Both the regimes in the north and the south had little tolerance for antiwar protests or any other kind of dissent. In the case of North Vietnam, if there were public protests, news of them never reached the outside world. The Communist regime would probably have crushed demonstrations of dissent with overwhelming force. Even public expressions of grief over the loss or injury of a loved one were discouraged. However, there were some North Vietnamese women who opposed the war, if only in silence. For example, author Karen Gottshang Turner wrote of a North Vietnamese woman who was opposed to the war: "She hated the socialism and the 'peasants who run the government.' . . . Sent by her university to support the war, . . . she resented having to go out of the city to work in boring, dirty jobs [instead of continuing her studies]." [69]

Protest was more visible in South Vietnam. The protests of the Xa Loi, a sect of Buddhists, were the most organized public dissent against the South Vietnamese government, and the one group where the participation of women was most significant. Buddhist doctrine considered men and women to be equal; women, both as nuns and as unordained believers, thus took an active part in street protests. The Xa Loi escalated war tensions with perhaps the most dramatic and horrible form of protest available—self-immolation (suicide by setting oneself on fire). Over the course of about three years, both monks and nuns immolated themselves in protest of the South Vietnamese government's mistreatment of Buddhists. Historian Stanley Karnow witnessed part of the immolation of Buddhist nun Thanh Quang on May 29, 1966. Karnow wrote, "She assumed the lotus position as one friend doused her with gasoline. Then she lighted a match, immediately exploding into flame. . . . By the time I arrived, her body was still erect, the hands clasped in prayer."[70] She was one of several nuns to commit suicide in this way in the course of a month.

Protest in America

Over time the Vietnam War became the least popular war in the history of the United States, and at home American women took a central role in protests against the war. Women were involved from the beginning of the antiwar movement.

The earliest protests by women against the war evolved out of college

Buddhist nun Thanh Quang burns after setting herself on fire in an act of protest against the policies of the South Vietnamese government.

Protesting the War

Women Strike for Peace was the first women's group to stage mass protests against the Vietnam War.

women; it was initially focused on extending civil rights to African Americans in the Deep South, but it came out against the Vietnam War in 1966. Its members were particularly active in supporting and demonstrating for African American men who resisted the military draft.

Another group, Students for a Democratic Society (SDS), was founded in 1962 and soon became the most recognizable antiwar student group, although it was involved in other issues too. Although SDS had many female members, women were mostly excluded from the leadership of SDS. They participated in demonstrations, but within the organization were relegated to traditional roles, such as office work and domestic duties, as the men tended to assume control. However, one woman, Bernardine Dohrn, was one of the most influential SDS members. She became the interorganizational secretary of SDS in 1968, responsible for fostering the growth of SDS at colleges across the country. She described herself at that time as a revolutionary Communist. Roman Tymchystyn, a student at Kent State University in Ohio in 1970, recalled her as "very strong-willed, very tough."[71]

Women Strike for Peace

Unlike SNCC and SDS, Women Strike for Peace (WSP) was focused exclusive-

campus politics about 1964. During this time some college students began to demonstrate in favor of equal rights for African Americans and free speech. The Student Nonviolent Coordinating Committee (SNCC) was one of the earliest campus organizations, formed in 1960 by idealistic young men and ly on the antiwar movement and was the first women's group to energetically seek an end to the war. WSP was established in Washington, D.C., in 1961, with general pacifist goals including bans on nuclear testing. As early as 1965 WSP was part of campus protests in Berkeley, California, against the Vietnam War, which it now took to be its focus. WSP members protested the manufacture of napalm, the material in American fire bombs, by trying to block shipments of the material from a chemical plant in California. They protested against this specific type of weapon because it had caused horrifying injuries to many Vietnamese women and children. Twenty-five hundred WSP protesters demonstrated at the Pentagon in January 1966.

In its early days WSP was a very loose organization, and its total membership is unknown to this day. WSP rarely had more than a few thousand women in its demonstrations, but the number of women involved with WSP seems to have been many times larger. Some indication of the size of the organization can be realized by the results of a postcard-writing campaign to President Johnson. He received one hundred thousand postcards in December 1965 from WSP members, demanding peace in Vietnam. It is doubtful each card came from a different WSP member, but the total still indicates involvement by a large number of women. The card-writing campaign did not have much influence on Johnson's war policy, but it was a first step by many women who had never involved themselves in the political process before, except perhaps as voters. This foreshadowed an increase in female political activism that eventually expanded beyond just antiwar issues.

Women Celebrities Oppose the War

The tide of female opposition to the war spread from students and other activists to celebrities. Until early 1967 very few celebrities had come out against the war. Many were supportive of the war policies and had demonstrated that support by visiting or entertaining the troops in South Vietnam.

The creation of Another Mother for Peace (AMP) in March 1967 by fifteen women from the film industry was the first example of mass activism against the war by female entertainers. The first major celebrity to take a visible position with AMP was Donna Reed, a film and television star with an Oscar to her credit. Despite her membership in the Republican Party, which favored the war, Reed campaigned for peace candidate Eugene McCarthy, a Democratic candidate for president in 1968. Other celebrities to back AMP included Debbie

Reynolds, Joanne Woodward, and Patty Duke. Apart from its celebrity power, AMP also had a way with words. It came up with perhaps the most famous peace slogan of the war: "War is not healthy for children and other living things."[72]

Also occurring in 1968 was the march of the Jeanette Rankin Brigade, supported by celebrity women. This was another WSP action, inspired by Jeanette Rankin, the eighty-seven-year-old former Montana congresswoman who had voted against the entry of the United States into both world wars. Despite her age, Rankin was at the head of five thousand demonstrators as they marched to the Capitol Building in Washington, D.C., on the opening day of Congress, January 15, 1968. Rankin was joined by singers Judy Collins and Diahann Carroll and actress Joanne Woodward. Most of the women were not allowed to enter the Capitol grounds, but Rankin, Coretta Scott King, and three others met with Vice President Hubert Humphrey that same day to formally press for peace.

Other celebrity women worked for peace in their own ways. Folksinger Joan Baez exemplified the many ways celebrities could take action. One of her earliest moves was to publicly refuse to pay the part of her federal income taxes she calculated went to the maintenance of the military. This was a symbolic gesture, since federal authorities impounded her assets to get the money anyway. With two other women, she posed for antidraft posters in 1967 bearing the caption "Girls Say Yes to Boys Who Say No." That same year she was arrested for helping men resist the draft. She went to a federal prison for this but was unrepentant, characterizing the minimum security facility as "the equivalent of a girl's summer camp."[73] Like many other celebrity women, Baez spoke against the war, sang against the war, and marched against it as well.

Several celebrity women went to North Vietnam to dramatize the horrors being inflicted on the people there by the American air bombardment. In July 1972, actress Jane Fonda went to Hanoi, where she remained for several weeks. Earlier, Joan Baez had gone there as did two female novelists, Susan Sontag and Mary McCarthy. Sontag was uncritical of the North Vietnamese, attributing their lack of free speech and cultural life to American oppression. McCarthy cast a more critical eye on the North Vietnamese during her trip in 1968, but she too was sympathetic to the Communists to some extent. All of these visits, particularly Fonda's, were controversial in the United States. To this day there are many who refer to her by the epithet "Hanoi Jane" and consider her guilty of treason against the United States for her

Jeanette Rankin

Montana Republican Jeanette Rankin was the first woman to serve in the U.S. House of Representatives and was one of the most committed pacifists ever to hold political office in the United States.

Rankin served only two two-year terms in Congress. She was elected for the first time in 1916, as World War I raged. When Congress voted to declare war against Germany in 1917, Rankin was one of fifty members of the House to vote against the declaration. Her vote, a matter of conscience, was unpopular, and she was not reelected in 1919. In 1940 she was again elected to Congress. She was the only member of either house of Congress to vote against declaring war on Japan on December 8, 1941. She was reviled throughout the country for this vote and left Congress at the end of her term.

Rankin continued to lead an active public life. She was in her eighties when America intervened in Vietnam; the conflict appalled her. She opposed Lyndon Johnson in his run for president in 1964; she thought he was a warmonger (one who stirs up a war for no good reason). In Rhodri Jeffrey-Jones's *Peace Now!* she is quoted as declaring that she "wanted to go back to Congress to vote against a third war." Her health precluded this, but she did march at the head of the Jeanette Rankin Brigade. She continued to work in the antiwar movement until 1972 at the age of ninety-two. Jeanette Rankin passed away in 1973 as America was withdrawing the last of its troops from Vietnam.

Nearly ninety years old, Jeanette Rankin (center, wearing glasses) marches in Washington, D.C., to protest the war in 1968.

activities in support of the North Vietnamese.

Mistreatment of POWs became an issue that attracted the involvement of women. Sybil Stockdale, the wife of POW James Stockdale, became frustrated with American government inaction on the issue, so in June 1969 she formed the National League of Families of American Prisoners in Southeast Asia. The organization's goals were to get a complete accounting of the prisoners, to assure proper treatment of the prisoners, and to gain their earliest possible release.

Jane Fonda

Of all the American celebrities who protested against the Vietnam War, Jane Fonda is probably the most controversial. Fonda, the winner of two Academy Awards for Best Actress, became involved in a variety of activist movements starting in 1970, including advocacy for Native Americans and for the Black Panther Party, a radical African American group. She kept her interest in these groups for some time, but by 1971 her primary focus was against the war in Vietnam.

In December 1970 the United States mounted a heavy bombing campaign against Hanoi and the area around it. Fonda reacted to what she considered a war crime by deciding to be a witness to the destruction. In July 1972 Fonda flew to Hanoi. She met with a few American POWS, made broadcasts over Radio Hanoi, and posed with an antiaircraft gun. Her radio speeches, and especially her public antagonism for the POWs, whom she branded as war criminals in the broadcasts, inflamed American public opinion against her. She came to be known by her detractors as "Hanoi Jane." In the end, Fonda, though still controversial and eternally branded a traitor by some, has come to be seen by many as one of the most important antiwar advocates.

The most controversial celebrity to protest the war, Jane Fonda sings an antiwar song to troops in Hanoi in 1972.

The administration of President Richard Nixon encouraged the group publicly, though it did virtually nothing to assist them behind the scenes. However, the group helped bring the pressure of world opinion against both the Nixon administration and the North Vietnamese, which may have accelerated the process of freeing the POWs.

Women in Congress

Early in the period of American intervention in Vietnam, American women had very little influence in Washington, D.C. There were only eleven female congressional representatives in the Ninetieth Congress, which ran from 1967 to 1969, and one female senator, Margaret Chase Smith of Maine. Smith supported the policies of the administration, though she had thought it a mistake to get involved in Vietnam in the first place. In the House of Representatives, Patsy Mink from Hawaii, the first Asian American woman to serve in Congress, and Edith Green from Oregon were the only women to oppose the war during that session of Congress. The other women, along with the vast majority of their male colleagues in the House, supported the war.

Beginning in 1970 WSP members began trying to end the war by turning Congress against it. They also had an interest in a broader set of issues that came to be known as feminism. In its simplest definition, feminism embodies equal rights for women, whether it relates to access to birth control, access to economic opportunity, equal pay for equal work, or equal rights before the law. WSP supported the aspirations of its women members by supporting women running for Congress. The first woman representative to take a leadership role in congressional opposition to the war was Bella Abzug. A member of WSP, Abzug wanted the emerging feminism to exert real legislative power. Women rallied behind Abzug in 1970 when she ran for Congress. She won, and took the lead in Congress in attempting to establish a date for withdrawal of American troops from Vietnam. By 1972 women such as Abzug, Mink, Shirley Chisholm, and Ellen Grasso were at the front of a wave in Congress that was moving to end funding for the war. Their efforts were crucial to the eventual end of American involvement in Vietnam.

Violence and Women in the Antiwar Movement

Women demonstrators sometimes participated in violent incidents relating to protests and sometimes were the victims of violence by police and others. The antiwar movement existed in a state of confrontation. Rallies and demonstrations sometimes turned into riots, especially when students were involved; rioters caused property damage and some injuries. Many times protesters were arrested, sometimes peacefully and sometimes despite violent resistance. Protesters and bystanders were frequently hit by tear gas, and police beat protesters with billy clubs. Violence was often serious but it was rarely life-threatening.

One notorious exception cost two young women their lives. Anger among antiwar activists and police authorities alike reached a crescendo in early May 1970, when the Americans attacked Cambodia across the Vietnamese border, where Viet Cong were based. Students on campuses across the country held massive protests. In Ohio, Governor Rhodes denounced the student demonstrators on state university campuses as "worse than Nazis, worse than Communists, worse than the Ku Klux Klan. They're the worst type of people we have in America."[74] He sent the Ohio National Guard to Kent State University, where hundreds of students, perhaps a third of them women, had been demonstrating and disrupting the campus. On May 4, in an encounter which remains confused to this day, four students were killed on campus by panicky or intentional National Guard gunfire, and nine others wounded. Two of the dead students were young women, Allison Krause and Sandy Scheuer.

At least one other American woman died in protest of the war; she followed the example of Xa Loi Buddhists. Alice Herz, an eighty-two-year-old Quaker and grandmother, immolated herself on a street corner in Detroit, Michigan, on March 16, 1965, to protest the war in Vietnam. A devoted pacifist, she took this drastic step to draw attention to her convictions against the war. She was the first of several self-immolation protests in the United States, though she was the only woman to commit suicide in this way.

A few women committed terrorist violence against others in pursuit of antiwar goals. The most radical group was known variously as the Weatherman, the Weathermen, and the Weather Underground. The Weathermen, a militant spinoff of SDS, had a membership of about three dozen revolutionaries; twelve were women. Among its founders was prominent SDS member Bernardine Dohrn. Other women involved were Kathy Boudin, Cathy Wilkerson, and Diana Oughton. In 1969 they incited the "Days of Rage" riot in Chicago, which resulted in wanton destruction of downtown businesses. Between 1970 and 1975 they set off about two dozen bombs in such places as the U.S. Senate barbershop and the New York Police Department. None of these bombs caused personal injury, but the wave of terrorism alienated others in the antiwar movement. Oughton eventually died with two others in a bomb explosion. The other women hid from the FBI and police for many years, but all eventually turned themselves in or were caught.

Allison Krause and Sandy Scheuer

It was shocking for most of America to hear of the student injuries and deaths at Kent State University, on May 4, 1970, in Ohio. Two young women, Allison Krause and Sandy Scheuer, were among the dead.

Krause, nineteen, participated in most of the antiwar demonstrations on the Kent State campus. Had she not been shot, her moment of fame might have been two days before, when she went to a young National Guard soldier on the campus and placed a flower in the muzzle of his rifle. James A. Michener, in *Kent State: What Happened and Why*, quoted her comment to the soldier: "Flowers are better than bullets."

In the late morning of May 4, Krause and her boyfriend were among students who taunted Ohio National Guard troops as they moved to break up the latest demonstration. Suddenly, the National Guard began firing. Although Krause took cover behind a car, she was shot in the upper body and died soon after arriving at the hospital.

Sandy Scheuer, twenty, took no part in the antiwar protests at the campus. She casually observed the demonstration for a few minutes, then headed for her next class. She was shot in the head, dying instantly. Michener assessed her as apolitical and well loved by her friends. He called her death "pure accident, inexplicable and unjustified."

On May 4, 1970, Ohio National Guard troops opened fire on an antiwar demonstration at Kent State University, killing four students.

The Protest Movement in Australia

Australia, America's most important ally in Vietnam, also developed a vigorous protest movement, though with much less violence. Women were the first organizers of opposition to the war, and began protests against the war as soon as Australians became involved. The beginnings of this opposition in Australia can be traced to the Women's International League for Peace and Freedom (WILPF).

The WILPF was founded in 1920 by an American woman, and was still active in many countries in 1960 when Margaret Holmes, then fifty-one, started up a branch in Mosman, Australia. This was the first branch of WILPF in Australia. There were soon about twenty members of the chapter, mainly suburban women with college degrees. Although Australia did not begin to get involved in Vietnam until 1962, the Mosman members of WILPF were aware of the conflict there by 1961 and viewed it with alarm. As the Australian government prepared the public for intervention in Vietnam, the Mosman women published advertisements in the newspapers, challenging government claims that force was the only way to stop communism in Asia. These advertisements first appeared on August 15, 1964, immediately after the Tonkin Gulf Incident. The ads continued for some time; one such ad, placed in a Sydney newspaper, reads as follows:

We are women in mourning.

We are mourning the youths who will lose their lives as conscripts [draftees] on overseas service.

We are mourning the youths who will be trained to kill their brother man.

We are mourning the loss of the individual's right to decide how best to serve his country.

Let us work for non-violent solutions of world problems.

Let us train our sons for LIFE not DEATH.[75]

The WILPF vocally opposed their government's actions in Vietnam as soon as they began.

Australian women also opposed the mandatory enlistment of young men into the Australian army. To show their disapproval, a group called Save Our Sons (SOS) was set up by fifteen women in Sydney in mid-May 1965, just two weeks after Australian prime minister Robert Menzies announced that Australian troops would go to Vietnam. Another group spontaneously formed under the same name in Melbourne, though it had no organizers in common. By the end of 1965 SOS had members, all women, in every Australian state. Despite the name, the movement was not limited to the mothers of draft-age males; the women in the organization covered every part of the political spectrum. In fact, many had no sons at all.

SOS women used a variety of tactics to oppose conscription and to exert influence politically. Perhaps the most strategic tactic was the Melbourne group's practice of advertising lectures on topics having nothing to do with the war. These midday lectures were designed to appeal to housewives with leisure time. In the middle of the presentation, there would be an intermission of the main topic. The emphasis would shift to a discussion on whether conscription was necessary. By this process, the Melbourne SOS reached many women who would never have attended specifically antidraft rallies.

The SOS women also had smart solutions to outwit authorities who tried to hinder them during rallies. In one instance, the government confiscated antiwar placards during a vigil in the capital of Canberra. The reaction of the women was to mark up paper shopping bags with their slogans, as the government never thought to take those away. The bags could be flashed like placards at the right time. They also learned to post antiwar signs around town during the early evening, when many people were about and their own activity would not stand out to attract police to remove the signs. In contrast to their defiance of authority in these ways, SOS members made a conscious effort to control their demeanor. All demonstrations were conducted without raucous or insulting calls, and the women maintained a dignified appearance.

The SOS members also engaged in civil disobedience, the purposeful breaking of laws to make a political point. One member, Jean MacLean, said, "Filling in false registration forms [for conscription] was [one] of our favorite pastimes. They didn't have [computers to check identity], and we used to register cats, dogs, [Prime Minister] Menzies, [Nazi leader Adolf] Hitler . . . [which] held up their system a lot and helped our cause."[76] At the same time, SOS began actively counseling potential conscripts on alternatives to military service. One of the most important alternatives, as in America, was to become a conscientious objector. Conscientious objectors asked to be exempted from combat, or even enlistment, because they objected to war as a matter of conscience or deeply held religious belief. The SOS retained attorneys to assist those seeking conscientious objector status, and ministers to counsel them.

Reaction in Australia to Escalation

As more Australian troops went to South Vietnam, the women's opposition groups became more active. In the fall of 1965 the WILPF hung one banner off a cliff at the mouth of Sydney Harbor that said "YOU GO TO AN UNJUST WAR" so that those on board one ship could see it as they went to sea. Two WILPF demonstrators chained themselves to the dockyard gates when another ship was due to sail in April 1966; they were cut free and then arrested, but released without charges.

For a time in 1966 the women in these organizations may have felt that they were standing in the path of a rising tide, as popularity for involvement in the war increased. More than once, demonstrators were outnumbered ten to one or more by prowar activists. The membership of SOS and WILPF did not waver, however. They kept the matter of the war in the public debate, and perhaps because they never resorted to violence, they managed to be heard, even if many rejected their message.

The tide of public opinion in Australia slowly turned. By August 1969 the prowar position was no longer held by a majority of the people. Demonstrations by SOS, WILPF, and other groups involving both men and women grew larger throughout 1970 and 1971.

Perhaps the most celebrated event of the women's anticonscription movement in Australia was the Fairlea Five incident. Five SOS women advocated resistance to the Australian National Service Act outside a conscription center in Melbourne just before Easter in 1971. It was against the law to encourage potential conscripts to refuse conscription, which was itself a crime. SOS groups had done this many times, and women had been arrested and fined for so doing in the past. This time, though, someone in the government decided to take a hard line; the women were jailed in Fairlea Prison just before the Easter weekend, and locked up for two weeks. This was a miscalculation by the government, because it turned the women, who among them had twenty-five children, into political celebrities. One of the women, Jean MacLean, recalled, "People all over Australia cancelled their Easter holidays and had huge vigils . . . outside the jail and a twenty-four hour [work] stoppage on the wharf; it was in every paper, and photographs of all the poor little children without their [mommies] at Easter."[77] In short, the government had created a public relations disaster for itself.

By 1972 the antiwar movement was winding down as Australia withdrew the last of its troops in South Vietnam, but the efforts of women had a lasting impact on the nature of Australian society. Their

Antiwar protesters in Sydney, Australia, demonstrate in 1966. Women were extremely active in Australia's protest movement throughout the war.

social and political influence in opposing the war empowered many Australian women to take the next step, as they sought a greater voice and larger roles in the whole society. Jean MacLean and another SOS activist, Joan Coxsedge, later became members of Australia's parliament, while Margaret Reynolds, another SOS member, eventually became a senator. Their status was symbolic of the ways in which the Vietnam War changed Australia and the roles of women.

Notes

Chapter 1:
The Vietnamese Home Fronts

1. Quoted in Susan Sheehan, *Ten Vietnamese.* New York: Alfred A. Knopf, 1967, p. 24.
2. Quoted in Sheehan, *Ten Vietnamese*, pp. 140–41.
3. Quoted in Harry Maurer, *Strange Ground: Americans in South Vietnam 1945–1975.* New York: Henry Holt, 1989, p. 323.
4. Quoted in Philip Bigler, *Hostile Fire: The Life and Death of First Lieutenant Sharon Lane.* Arlington, VA: Vandamere, 1996, p. 130.
5. Siobhan McHugh, *Minefields and Miniskirts: Australian Women and the Vietnam War.* New York: Doubleday, 1993, p. 13.
6. Stanley Karnow, *Vietnam: A History.* New York: Penguin, 1997, p. 440.
7. Quoted in Maurer, *Strange Ground*, p. 493.
8. Quoted in McHugh, *Minefields and Miniskirts*, p. 52.
9. Quoted in Maurer, *Strange Ground*, p. 474.
10. Quoted in Edith Lederer, "My First War," in Tad Bartimus et al., *War Torn: Stories of War from the Women Reporters Who Covered Vietnam.* New York: Random House, 2002, p. 170.
11. Quoted in Maurer, *Strange Ground*, p. 107.
12. Quoted in Maurer, *Strange Ground*, p. 257.
13. Quoted in Bigler, *Hostile Fire*, p. 125.
14. Quoted in Bigler, *Hostile Fire*, p. 125.
15. Quoted in Maurer, *Strange Ground*, p. 141.
16. Liz Trotta, *Fighting for Air: In the Trenches with Television News.* New York: Simon & Schuster, 1991, p. 94.
17. Quoted in Sheehan, *Ten Vietnamese*, pp. 35–36.
18. Denby Fawcett, "Walking Point," in Bartimus, et al., *War Torn*, p. 20.
19. Quoted in Maurer, *Strange Ground*, pp. 516–17.
20. Jon M. Van Dyke, *North Vietnam's Strategy for Survival.* Palo Alto, CA: Pacific Books, 1972, p. 95.
21. Quoted in Karen Gottschang Turner, *Even the Women Must Fight: Memories of the War from*

North Vietnam. New York: John Wiley, 1998, pp. 88–89.

22. Van Dyke, *North Vietnam's Strategy for Survival*, p. 97.

23. Quoted in Turner, *Even the Women Must Fight*, p. 76.

24. Van Dyke, *North Vietnam's Strategy for Survival*, p. 97.

Chapter 2: Medical Personnel and Welfare Workers in Vietnam

25. Quoted in Turner, *Even the Women Must Fight*, p. 139.

26. Albert Marrin, *America and Vietnam: The Elephant and the Tiger.* New York: Penguin Books, 1992, p. 107.

27. Quoted in Turner, *Even the Women Must Fight*, p. 140.

28. Quoted in Keith Walker, *A Piece of My Heart: The Stories of Twenty-Six American Women Who Served in Vietnam.* Novato, CA: Presidio, 1985, p. 98.

29. Quoted in Maurer, *Strange Ground*, pp. 280–81.

30. Quoted in Walker, *A Piece of My Heart*, p. 264.

31. Quoted in McHugh, *Minefields and Miniskirts*, p. 19.

32. Bigler, *Hostile Fire*, p. 70.

33. Quoted in Maurer, *Strange Ground*, p. 405.

34. Quoted in Walker, *A Piece of My*

Heart, p. 210.

35. Quoted in McHugh, *Minefields and Miniskirts*, p. 15.

36. Ann Bryan Mariano, "Vietnam Is Where I Found My Family," in Bartimus, et al., *War Torn*, p. 45.

37. Quoted in McHugh, *Minefields and Miniskirts*, p. 44.

38. Quoted in Walker, *A Piece of My Heart*, p. 187.

Chapter 3: Keeping Spirits Up

39. Quoted in McHugh, *Minefields and Miniskirts*, p. 40.

40. Truong Nhu Tang with David Chanoff and Doan Van Toai, *A Viet Cong Memoir: An Inside Account of the Vietnam War and Its Aftermath.* New York: Harcourt Brace Jovanovich, 1985, p. 166.

41. Quoted in Turner, *Even the Women Must Fight*, p. 47.

42. Quoted in Walker, *A Piece of My Heart*, p. 126.

43. Quoted in Walker, *A Piece of My Heart*, p. 89.

44. Quoted in McHugh, *Minefields and Miniskirts*, pp. 26–27.

45. Frank Coffey, *Always Home: Fifty Years of the USO—the Official Photographic History.* New York: Brassey's, 1991, p. 92.

46. Quoted in McHugh, *Minefields and Miniskirts*, p. 28.

47. Quoted in Walker, *A Piece of My*

Heart, p. 30.

48. Quoted in Walker, *A Piece of My Heart,* p. 65.

Chapter 4: War Correspondents

49. Quoted in Fawcett, "Walking Point," pp. 4–5.

50. Quoted in Trotta, *Fighting for Air,* p. 58.

51. Tracy Wood, "Spies, Lovers, and Prisoners of War," in Bartimus, et al., *War Torn,* pp. 224–25.

52. Jurate Kazickas, "These Hills Called Khe Sanh," in Bartimus, et al., *War Torn,* p. 134.

53. Kate Webb, "Highpockets," in Bartimus, et al., *War Torn,* p. 62.

54. Trotta, *Fighting for Air,* p. 125.

55. Gloria Emerson, in "Introduction," in Bartimus, et al., *War Torn,* p. xix.

56. Fawcett, "Walking Point," p. 29.

57. Quoted in Horst Faas and Tim Page, eds., *Requiem: By the Photographers Who Died in Vietnam and Indochina.* New York: Random House, 1997, p. 136.

58. Kazickas, "These Hills Called Khe Sanh," p. 146.

59. Quoted in Maurer, *Strange Ground,* pp. 238–39.

60. Trotta, *Fighting for Air,* p. 161.

Chapter 5: Women Combatants

61. Quoted in Turner, *Even the Women Must Fight,* pp. 126–27.

62. Quoted in Turner, *Even the Women Must Fight,* p. 113.

63. Harrison Salisbury, *Behind the Lines—Hanoi: December 23–January 7.* New York: Harper & Row, 1967, p. 140.

64. Quoted in Marrin, *America and Vietnam,* pp. 95–96.

65. Quoted in Turner, *Even the Women Must Fight,* pp. 35–36.

66. Quoted in Marguerite Higgins, *Our Vietnam Nightmare.* New York: Harper & Row, 1965, p. 64.

67. Quoted in McHugh, *Minefields and Miniskirts,* p.78.

68. Quoted in Walker, *A Piece of My Heart,* p. 112.

Chapter 6: Protesting the War

69. Turner, *Even the Women Must Fight,* p. 84.

70. Karnow, *Vietnam,* p. 449.

71. James A. Michener, *Kent State: What Happened and Why.* New York: Random House, 1971, p. 91.

72. Quoted in Rhodri Jeffrey-Jones, *Peace Now!* New Haven, CT: Yale University Press, 1999, p. 158.

73. Quoted in Jeffrey-Jones, *Peace Now!* p. 160.

74. Quoted in A.J. Langguth, *Our Vietnam: The War 1954–1975.* New York: Simon & Schuster,

2000, p. 569.

75. J. Finley, paid advertisement, *North Shore Times*, Sydney, Australia, December 2, 1964, p. 49.

76. Quoted in McHugh, *Minefields and Miniskirts*, p. 209.

77. Quoted in McHugh, *Minefields and Miniskirts*, p. 224.

For Further Reading

Books

Barry Denenberg, *Voices from Vietnam.* New York: Scholastic, 1995. Provides a series of short statements by people in Vietnam during the war, telling of their experiences in their own words.

Philip Gavin, *The Fall of Vietnam.* San Diego, CA: Lucent Books, 2003. Describes the aftermath of the Vietnam War and the effect on the Vietnamese people.

Denis J. Hauptly, *In Vietnam.* New York: Atheneum, 1985. Discusses Vietnamese history from the ancient past up to American involvement in the Vietnam War.

Deborah Kent, *The Vietnam Women's Memorial.* Chicago: Childrens Press, 1995. A short book describing the design, construction, and dedication of a memorial to women who served in Vietnam during the war.

Don Lawson, *The United States in the Vietnam War.* New York: Thomas Y. Crowell, 1981. A detailed account of American involvement in the war.

Edward E. Rice, *Ten Religions of the East.* New York: Four Winds, 1978. A discussion of Eastern religions, including the Cao Dai faith indigenous to Vietnam.

Lynda Van Devanter, *Home Before Morning: The Story of an Army Nurse in Vietnam.* New York: Warner, 1983. Autobiographical story of a nurse's experiences in Vietnam.

James A. Warren, *Portrait of a Tragedy: America and the Vietnam War.* New York: Lothrop, Lee & Shepard Books, 1990. Describes American involvement in Vietnam during the war.

Andrew West, *The Vietnam War 1956–1973.* Oxford, UK: Osprey, 2002. A brief, well-balanced, and accurate summary of the events of the Vietnam War.

Charles Wills, *The Tet Offensive.* Englewood Cliffs, NJ: Silver Burdett, 1989. Describes the most destructive series of battles of the Vietnam War.

Web Sites

Alan Canfora (http://alancanfora.com). This Web site is authored by one of the students injured by the National Guard gunfire at Kent State on May 4, 1970. It provides information on the victims and what happened that day.

Mike and Kendra's Web Site
(www.may41970. com). Includes photos and some details of the four students killed at Kent State by the Ohio National Guard, as well as other information about the incident.

Kim Foundation International
(www.kimfoundation.com/en). This is the entry page for the Kim Foundation International, established by Phan Thi Kim Phuc to help children injured in wars, as she was in South Vietnam. It includes links to her story and to photos.

The Vietnam Experience (www.vietnamexp.com/Links/nam_women. htm). This Web page gives a number of links to other sites about women in various roles in Vietnam.

Works Consulted

Books

Tad Bartimus et al., *War Torn: Stories of War from the Women Reporters Who Covered Vietnam.* New York: Random House, 2002. Essays by nine female reporters in Vietnam during the war.

Philip Bigler, *Hostile Fire: The Life and Death of First Lieutenant Sharon Lane.* Arlington, VA: Vandamere, 1996. Biography of the only American female nurse to be killed by hostile fire in South Vietnam.

Denise Chong, *The Girl in the Picture.* New York: Viking Penguin, 1999. The biography of napalm victim Phan Thi Kim Phuc.

Frank Coffey, *Always Home: Fifty Years of the USO—the Official Photographic History.* New York: Brassey's, 1991. Captioned photos and some text, covering the USO from 1941. Includes material and photographs relating to women who performed for or worked with the USO.

Horst Faas and Tim Page, eds., *Requiem: By the Photographers Who Died in Vietnam and Indochina.* New York: Random House, 1997. Photographs by photographers killed during the war, as well as short essays about them.

Carol Gelderman, *Mary McCarthy: A Life.* New York: St. Martin's, 1988. A biography of Mary McCarthy, including material on her trips to Vietnam.

William A. Gordon, *The Fourth of May: Killings and Coverups at Kent State.* New York: Prometheus Books, 1990. A review of the circumstances surrounding the deaths and injuries of students at Kent State at the hands of the Ohio National Guard.

Fred Lawrence Guiles, *Jane Fonda: An Actress in Her Time.* New York: Doubleday, 1982. A biography of Jane Fonda.

Marguerite Higgins, *Our Vietnam Nightmare.* New York: Harper & Row, 1965. A scathing look at how things were going wrong for the Americans early in their involvement in the Vietnam War.

Rhodri Jeffrey-Jones, *Peace Now!* New Haven, CT: Yale University Press, 1999. Includes an extensive discussion of the involvement of American women in the antiwar movement.

Hannah Josephson, *Jeannette Rankin: First Lady in Congress.* New York:

Bobbs-Merrill, 1974. A biography of the first woman U.S. congressional representative. Jeanette Rankin was famous for her antiwar stance in two world wars, and resumed her activism during the Vietnam War.

Stanley Karnow, *Vietnam: A History*. New York: Penguin, 1997. A history of Vietnam, culminating with a detailed look at the war.

Harvey W. Kushner, *Encyclopedia of Terrorism*. Thousand Oaks, CA: Sage, 2003. Includes entries for the Weather Underground/Weatherman and for some of the women involved in it.

Stanley I. Kutler, ed., *Encyclopedia of the Vietnam War*. New York: Charles Scribner's Sons, 1996. A collection of brief articles on every facet of the Vietnam War, including the protest movement in America.

A.J. Langguth, *Our Vietnam: The War 1954–1975*. New York: Simon & Schuster, 2000. A history of the Vietnam War.

Stanley Robert Larsen and James Lawton Collins Jr., *Allied Participation in Vietnam*. Washington, DC: Department of the Army, 1985. A discussion of the scope of involvement of nations allied with the United States and South Vietnam against Communist insurgency.

Albert Marrin, *America and Vietnam: The Elephant and the Tiger*. New York: Penguin Books, 1992. A somewhat argumentative but well-written discussion of the Vietnam War and its effect on the Vietnamese and Americans.

Harry Maurer, *Strange Ground: Americans in South Vietnam 1945–1975*. New York: Henry Holt, 1989. Transcribed interviews with American men and women in various roles in South Vietnam.

Siobhan McHugh, *Minefields and Miniskirts: Australian Women and the Vietnam War*. New York: Doubleday, 1993. This book gives details about the involvement of Australian women in Vietnam during the war, and those who protested Australian involvement in the war. There is also some information on Vietnamese women.

James A. Michener, *Kent State: What Happened and Why*. New York: Random House, 1971. A detailed narrative of the Kent State tragedy, laced with Michener's opinions.

Lowell Robertssen, *Remembering the Women of the Vietnam War*. Eden Prairie, MN: Tessera, 1990. This book is a collection of poetry, inspired by the women in Vietnam during the war.

Carl Rollyson and Lisa Paddock, *Susan Sontag: The Making of an Icon*. New York: W. W. Norton, 2000. A biography of Susan Sontag, including information on her trip to North Vietnam.

Harrison Salisbury, *Behind the Lines—Hanoi: December 23–January 7*. New York: Harper & Row, 1967. Observations of a *New York Times* reporter, who spent two weeks in North Vietnam in 1966–1967.

Susan Sheehan, *Ten Vietnamese*. New York: Alfred A. Knopf, 1967. Transcribed interviews with Vietnamese in ten varied roles, including a peasant, a Viet Cong, a South Vietnamese soldier, and others.

James Bond Stockdale and Sybil B. Stockdale, *In Love and War: The Story of a Family's Ordeal and Sacrifice During the Vietnam Years*. New York: Harper & Row, 1984. An American prisoner of war and his wife tell the story of his captivity in North Vietnam and her relentless efforts to seek freedom for all the POWs.

Liz Trotta, *Fighting for Air: In the Trenches with Television News*. New York: Simon & Schuster, 1991. Autobiography of a female broadcast war correspondent.

Truong Nhu Tang with David Chanoff and Doan Van Toai, *A Viet Cong Memoir: An Inside Account of the Vietnam War and Its Aftermath*. New York: Harcourt Brace Jovanovich, 1985. The autobiography of a former Viet Cong activist and justice minister of the Provisional Revolutionary Government.

Karen Gottschang Turner, *Even the Women Must Fight: Memories of the War from North Vietnam*. New York: John Wiley, 1998. Details the contribution of North Vietnamese women to the war.

Jon M. Van Dyke, *North Vietnam's Strategy for Survival*. Palo Alto, CA: Pacific Books, 1972. An analysis of how North Vietnam managed its people and resources to cope with the extreme demands of the war.

Keith Walker, *A Piece of My Heart: The Stories of Twenty-Six American Women Who Served in Vietnam*. Novato, CA: Presidio, 1985. A series of interviews with American women who served in a variety of roles in South Vietnam during the war.

Periodical

J. Finley, paid advertisement, *North Shore Times*, Sydney, Australia, December 2, 1964. A political advertisement placed in a newspaper by the Sydney chapter of the Women's International League for Peace and Freedom.

Internet Sources

Bill McDonald, "Story of Raye," The Vietnam Experience. www.vietnamexp.com/morestories/MarthaRaye.htm. Details about Martha Raye in Vietnam.

Lorie Ritchie, "What Is Agent Orange?" Lyght Force, www.lyghtforce.com/HomeopathyOnline/issue5/articles/ritchie_orange.html. Provides a short description of the composition, use, and effects of Agent Orange, Agent Blue, and Agent White in Vietnam.

Matt Sollett, "Self-Immolation During the Vietnam Era," Angelfire, www.angelfire.com/nb/protest. Details on the self-immolation of Alice Herz.

United Services Organization, "USO Home Page," www.uso.org. This site includes some short essays on the history of the USO, as well as a listing of all of Bob Hope's tours and the entertainers who accompanied him on each tour.

Index

Picture Credits

꧁

Cover: National Archives
AP/Wide World Photos, 8, 33, 64, 74, 83, 88
© Bettmann/CORBIS, 13, 21, 22, 27, 34, 35, 39, 42, 48, 50, 59, 71, 78, 84, 87, 91, 95
Courtesy of Denby Fawcett, 58, 63

Getty Images, 67
Hulton/Archive by Getty Images, 53
National Archives, 29, 30, 47
© Christine Spengler/CORBIS, 18
Time Life Pictures/Getty Images, 16, 25, 73

About the Author

꧁

Mark Schynert is a freelance writer with a law degree and a master's degree in political science. Most of his nonfiction writing has focused on twentieth-century history. He lives in northern California with his wife, Susan, and their daughter, Kendra.